A PLUME BOOK

WENDY KNITS

WENDY D. JOHNSON is a lifelong knitter who has for the past three years maintained what many people consider the premier knitting blog (wendyknits.net), attracting more than three million visitors per month. She's produced designs for the knitting website Knitty.com, and has been quoted or featured in most of the major knitting magazines. She is currently the house designer for Knit Happens, the celebrated yarn shop located in her hometown of Alexandria, Virginia, and often teaches at knitting retreats around the country. When she isn't talking about knitting, dreaming about knitting, or actually knitting, she works for the Department of Labor's Employment Standards Administration.

Wendy Knits

My Never-Ending Adventures in Yarn

Wendy D. Johnson

A PLUME BOOK

PLUME
Published by Penguin Group
Penguin Group (USA) Inc., 375 Hudson Street, New York, New York 10014, U.S.A.
Penguin Group (Canada), 90 Eglinton Avenue East, Suite 700, Toronto, Ontario, Canada M4P 2Y3 (a division of Pearson Penguin Canada Inc.) • Penguin Books Ltd., 80 Strand, London WC2R 0RL, England • Penguin Ireland, 25 St. Stephen's Green, Dublin 2, Ireland (a division of Penguin Books Ltd.) • Penguin Group (Australia), 250 Camberwell Road, Camberwell, Victoria 3124, Australia (a division of Pearson Australia Group Pty. Ltd.) • Penguin Books India Pvt. Ltd., 11 Community Centre, Panchsheel Park, New Delhi – 110 017, India • Penguin Books (NZ), cnr Airborne and Rosedale Roads, Albany, Auckland 1310, New Zealand (a division of Pearson New Zealand Ltd.) • Penguin Books (South Africa) (Pty.) Ltd., 24 Sturdee Avenue, Rosebank, Johannesburg 2196, South Africa

Penguin Books Ltd., Registered Offices: 80 Strand, London WC2R 0RL, England

First published by Plume, a member of Penguin Group (USA) Inc.

First Printing, May 2006
10 9 8 7 6 5 4 3 2 1

Ⓟ REGISTERED TRADEMARK—MARCA REGISTRADA

LIBRARY OF CONGRESS CATALOGING-IN-PUBLICATION DATA

Johnson, Wendy D.
    Wendy knits : my never-ending adventures in yarn / by Wendy D. Johnson.
        p.   cm.
    "A Plume book."
    ISBN 0-452-28732-4
1. Knitting.   2. Knitting—Patterns.   3. Knitters (Persons)—Miscellanea.   I. Title.
    TT820.J57 2006
    746.43'2—dc22

                                                2005030004

Printed in the United States of America
Set in Bernhard Modern
Designed by Dianne Pinkowitz

BOOKS ARE AVAILABLE AT QUANTITY DISCOUNTS WHEN USED TO PROMOTE PRODUCTS OR SERVICES. FOR INFORMATION PLEASE WRITE TO PREMIUM MARKETING DIVISION, PENGUIN GROUP (USA) INC., 375 HUDSON STREET, NEW YORK, NEW YORK 10014.

To Lindsey-Brooke Hessa, Johanne Ländin, and Kristine Kirby
Webster, for their unfailing support and friendship,
and to the Wednesday Night Irregulars, just for being there

Contents

Acknowledgments	ix
List of Patterns	xi
1. I Knit, Therefore I Am	1
2. The Laws of Knitting	13
3. "Virtuality" versus Reality	31
4. Knitting and Others	47
5. Knitting for Charity	63
6. Why a Sock?	79
7. There's No Crying in Knitting!	93
8. Needles and Numbers	111
9. What Was I Thinking?	127
10. The Fiber Snob	145
11. What's a Peerie?	171
12. Putting a Spin on It	187
Abbreviations	201
Glossary of Terms	203
Resources	211

Acknowledgments

Thanks to Knit Happens, 127A North Washington Street, Alexandria, Virginia 22314 (www.knithappens.net) for supplying yarn for many of the projects contained herein.

Thanks to Lindsey-Brooke Hessa for knitting the sample catnip mice pictured herein.

Models: Aimee Houghton, Cindy Miller, Phyllis Marsh Schaeffer, Kristine Kirby Webster, Lucy the cat, and Axel the dog.

Photographs by Rich Webster Jr.

List of Patterns

Plain Old Dishcloth   15
Ribbed Dishcloth   15
Box Stitch Dishcloth   16
Fisherman's Rib Scarf   19
Scallop Scarf   20
Trellis Lace Scarf   21
Fir Cone Scarf   22
Easy One-Skein Hat   24
Vince Sweater   26
Lucky Tank Top   41
Lisa Ribbed Pullover   58
Excruciatingly Easy Garter Stitch Catnip Mouse   68
Sophisticated Cabled Catnip Mouse for the Debonair
    Cat-about-Town   70
Felted Pet Bed   75
Wendy's Generic Toe-Up Socks   87
Laura Pullover   106
Lucy Top   135
Melody Cabled Pullover   140
Lauren Tank   153
Grape Arbor Shawl   157
Ingrid Pullover   181
Silk Cell Phone Cozy   196
Fingerless Mitts   198

Chapter 1 • I Knit, Therefore I Am

I WAS BORN INTO A FIBER-FRIENDLY WORLD. My mother had quite a bit of artistic talent and was accomplished in all needlecrafts: knitting, sewing, and embroidery. Mom knitted two-color ski sweaters, cabled Aran sweaters, and beautiful baby clothes. She made Scandinavian-style mittens for my brother and me when we were small, with our names knitted in above the cuffs. I can remember clearly a pair that she designed and made for my brother—they had a silhouette of a bowlegged cowboy sitting on a fence knitted into the back of each hand. Another memorable Mom-knit was a beautiful lavender sweater and pleated skirt she knitted for me when I was just a tot. When I was a few years older she made me a lovely raspberry-colored wool suit. She knitted suits and jackets and sweaters for herself as well. I'm sure that she made more than one sweater for Dad, too, though the only one I can recall is a green Scandinavian ski sweater patterned with white reindeer that I think she made for him before they were married.

As a toddler, I loved to play with the bits of yarn that Mom saved from various projects. She kept all her yarn leftovers, neatly wound into balls, in a large cardboard box. I was fascinated by the various shapes, sizes, colors, and textures of these balls of yarn, and would happily play with them for hours. She kept all her knitting needles in a long cylindrical plastic case that had a lid that screwed on and off and I played with those too. I would carefully unscrew the lid and pour the needles out on the floor, marveling at the number and variety that could fit in the slim tube. There were straight needles in all different sizes, lengths, and colors, as well as a few sets of double-pointed needles, which seemed particularly mysterious and exotic to me, as I had no idea how they were used.

At some point, quite early on, Mom put yarn and needles in my hands. She cast on some stitches for me, showed me what to do, and away I went. I remember that at that time she had a book or magazine that contained a "how to knit" section with illustrations. I reinforced what I learned from Mom by mimicking what was going on in the illustrations, either because I did not yet know how to read, or did not yet read well enough to comprehend instructions written for an adult.

For a few years I was happy to knit doll blankets from my mother's leftover yarn. I made blankets in all colors and sizes and once even made a doll-sized sleeping bag. I made a crude little sweater for one of my brother's plastic toy dinosaurs and presented it to him. As I recall, he wasn't particularly impressed by my creation, but being in an expansive mood at the time, he put it on the dinosaur all the same.

When I was nine years old, I started pestering Mom because I wanted to knit a "real" sweater. She took me to a yarn shop and we picked out a pattern for a simple raglan crewneck pullover. And after much deliberation, I picked out the yarn I wanted to use: it was bright red worsted-weight wool.

That sweater took me five years to knit, but I did finally finish it, when I was fourteen years old. Mom wisely had me start out making a size large enough so that I could actually wear it when it was completed. I did wear it, and, surprisingly, it didn't look too bad.

Over the next few years, I knitted intermittently. Knitting was not my number one favorite pastime, but I did make a few (admittedly hideous) pullovers from cheap acrylic yarn of dubious quality bought at the dime store. My mother always encouraged my knitting, as she did all my creative endeavors. I have a fond memory of coming home from school one day as a young teenager, going up to my room, and finding laid out on my bed a complete set of knitting needles that she had bought for me that day. It was a wonderful feeling—I now had my own set of tools!

I was an artistic kid, and knitting fitted nicely in the rotation with the rest of the crafts in which I dabbled. I sketched, painted, and worked with clay. In addition to embroidery and sewing, at which I became pretty accomplished, I attempted weaving and making lace, with admittedly disastrous results in both cases. There was one ugly attempt at making paper from wood pulp that is best forgotten.

When I was eighteen years old and a freshman in college, I wanted to knit my boyfriend a sweater as a gift. I found a pattern for an Aran fisherman-knit sweater—and a fairly complicated one at that, with lots of cables and texture stitches. Up to this point I had never done anything but simple ribbing and stockinette stitch. But with the fearlessness (or stupidity?) of youth, I took the pattern to a local yarn shop and the shopkeeper helped me pick out the appropriate yarn (still acrylic, but a nice-quality acrylic this time). I cast on for the back that night and knitted the ribbing as quickly as I could. I was very eager to get into the body of the sweater and try out those pattern stitches.

But everything came to a screeching halt. How the heck do you make a cable? I tried it, failed at it, and ripped it out. Again, tried it, failed at it, and ripped it out. I was completely and utterly mystified! The pattern was written out in words and abbreviations—this was before charts became commonplace in knitting patterns. Looking back, I would probably have grasped the pattern much better had there been a chart, as I'm a very visual person. I simply could not comprehend what the directions meant and there was no one around I could ask. This was possibly the single most frustrating event in my life thus far.

I stubbornly kept trying, twisting, and torturing the offending stitches any and every way I could imagine. Working and ripping, again and again. And then, finally, I figured it out. The instructions suddenly made sense and the cables looked the way they ought to. It was like a lightbulb switching on. Ding! Bells were ringing, and I could have sworn I heard a choir singing the Alleluia Chorus from Handel's *Messiah*. It's been nearly thirty years, but I vividly remember the thrill of that moment and the heady rush of accomplishment I felt. There is nothing quite as satisfying as figuring out a puzzle on your own, without any help.

I think I stayed up all night knitting on that night of the Cable Epiphany. I was so delighted that I had turned an incomprehensible mishmash of abbreviations and hieroglyphics that were the written pattern into something recognizable as a cabled sweater that I simply couldn't stop. Watching the cables and texture form on my needles was utterly fascinating, and I kept going so I could see the pattern emerging in its entire three-dimensional splendor. In my enthusiasm, I finished the sweater very quickly. I then discovered that the nice lady in the yarn shop had sold me exactly double the amount of yarn I needed for the sweater. So, aglow with my success with the first Aran sweater, I turned around and made a second one, for me.

The boyfriend liked the sweater, so a few more followed. Some plain sweaters, some cabled sweaters. Even a Nordic-inspired color-work pullover in a repulsive bulky yarn in some (as I recall) less than lovely colors. I made myself another Aran sweater, a stunning complicated pattern, in beautiful natural-colored wool. And another one in a different, but still complicated pattern.

But knitting was still just an occasional hobby at this point—something I'd pick up and do every now and then, when I wasn't sewing or embroidering.

Then in the early 1980s I had a sort of knitting renaissance. After having done no knitting for a few months, I felt the urge to start a new knitting project. I went into a yarn shop that I had passed by but never entered, and was greeted by an extraordinary sight. There were skeins and skeins of different yarns in a rainbow of colors and a variety of weights and textures, and beautiful patterns that were written specifically for those yarns in the shop, each set of patterns strategically placed next to the yarns they were written for. I picked out a pattern for a cabled polo-neck pullover and bought the yarn for it, a lavender wool/mohair blend. As soon as I cast on for this sweater, I fell in love with knitting all over again.

Within six months I had a part-time job in that shop, ostensibly to supplement my income, but the truth was that I wanted, nay, needed to be near the yarn. And the 20 percent employee discount didn't hurt. The shop owner loved me: I'd buy yarn, knit it up over the weekend, and then wear the sweater when I came to work in the shop. I was a living, breathing advertisement, and a pretty good one at that.

Unfortunately, I had to quit that job after only a few months because I was spending more money than I made, thus defeating the purpose of having a second job. But the die was cast, the foundation was laid. I was hooked on knitting for good.

In 1984, the *Vogue Knitting* magazine was revived—it had ceased publication in the late 1960s. I subscribed, and waited anxiously for the first issue, which obligingly arrived on the eve of a major snowstorm. Over the next few days, happily snowbound, I pored through that magazine intently, reading the articles over and over and scrutinizing the designs. Admittedly, at that time most of the designs in *Vogue Knitting* were a tad too haute couture for me, like a design that had "stair steps" in the sleeve shaping, but they gave me lots of ideas. Ideas for slightly less "out there" designs I might try and ideas for yarns I could use. And I learned about techniques that I hadn't tried or even heard of.

It was through an advertisement in *Vogue Knitting*, I believe, that I found out about the Knitting Guild of America (TKGA). TKGA (now renamed the

Knitting Guild Association) is an organization that promotes the craft of knitting and provides educational services, including regional and national conventions. I joined the organization. I went to my first TKGA national convention in the mid-1980s, and actually met and interacted with other knitters socially—a first for me.

Up to this point, I was always a bit embarrassed and defensive about my knitting. Friends and acquaintances would usually make fun of me when I whipped out the needles in front of them. Knitting was an "old lady" pastime, they jeered. I was young and craved peer approval, so I stopped knitting in front of other people.

The convention was an eye-opener! I got to make friends and hang out with other knitters who were passionate about their craft. These were no typical old ladies! Sure, there were some grannies in the group, but most of these knitters, young and old, were energetic, dynamic individuals. A group of them (myself included) closed the bar in the hotel every night.

I took some classes from some now-famous designers and learned about more new techniques and types of knitting. I also had the opportunity to shop in a huge vendor market and discover even more fiber delights. Alpaca! Silk! Cashmere! A whole new world of fiber obsession had opened up for me.

I made some interesting discoveries about myself as well.

The first was that I have a somewhat odd knitting style. I suppose this is to be expected, given that I was largely self-taught. Most of my knitting up to this point was done in solitude. Apart from being taught by her, I don't remember ever really sitting and knitting with my mother. In fact, I couldn't tell you what her knitting style is, as I can't visualize her actually knitting. I do know, of course, that she knitted when I was a kid, and knitted a lot, but I only remember it vaguely. I guess knitting simply wasn't a group sport in our house. I was (and still am) an independent little cuss and always preferred to do things on my own without asking for guidance. So, no, I don't think we ever really sat down and knit together.

I also found out that there was more than one way to achieve a result. And that my way was not necessarily the best way. Up to this point I had assumed that the way I did something was how it was done, period. End of story.

I was at a knitting convention, taking a class about different ribbing techniques. The first thing we were told to do by the instructor was to cast on a number of stitches using the long-tail cast-on method, in preparation for learning the first technique. Everyone in the class whipped out their needles and nimbly cast on their stitches, manipulating the yarn . . . *using only one hand.*

I still bow my head in shame when I think about this. Up until this point I had been casting on stitches laboriously, using two hands. No wonder it took me forever. No wonder I hated casting on. I had figured out how to cast on from that book with pictures, many years ago, and did it the only way I could manage it as a small child with limited dexterity—with two hands. In the ensuing years, it had never occurred to me that there might be a better way of doing it. I just assumed that my way was the only way, so this was an eye-opener, a "wow" moment for me.

I cast surreptitious glances around the class, sure that everyone was pointing and whispering and sniggering behind their hands at me, but, miraculously, no one seemed to notice my pathetic cast-on attempts. Soon, I figured out the technique for one-handed long-tail cast-on in record time.

I guess this was a good life lesson. In the arrogance of youth I was blithely knitting along, thinking I knew what I was doing, and that I, of course, did it better than anyone else. And then I bumped up against reality. I came out of that experience a bit humbler, and a lot wiser. Since then I've always tried to remember that no matter what I do, there is always room for improvement, and there is always someone who can do it better.

But I did find out a good thing, too. While I may have an odd knitting style, I can knit pretty darn fast. Apart from casting on, that is. Self-taught was not necessarily a bad thing! I had figured out, on my own, the best and most comfortable and efficient way to hold my needles and devised a style that worked for me. On a few rare occasions I have run into someone with a similar knitting style, and it always surprises me. It's as though I've found a long-lost relative.

I've had people say to me, "Oh, you knit Continental." "You knit European." "You're a picker." "You're a thrower." Huh? None of these terms mean anything to me.

Nowadays I am often asked what knitting style I use by people who want to emulate it to improve their knitting speed. I never know what to answer, because I have no idea what to call my style. I'm left-handed and knit from the left needle onto the right needle. Some lefties do the opposite, though I've never seen one in action. I don't tension my yarn through my fingers but (horrors!) pick it up with each stitch. So I guess you could say that I am a Quasi-Leftie-Untensioned-Picker-Knitter.

And of course my odd knitting style was something else I used to feel self-conscious about when knitting in front of other people, but I've finally gotten over that. It works for me. I knit quickly and evenly and turn out pleasing final products. And I do this without, apparently, undue strain on my wrists and hands because I can usually knit for hours at a time without pain, unless I'm using a particularly rough yarn.

I've also successfully taught quite a few people to knit—both left-handers and right-handers. When teaching new knitters I have always stressed that they should hold the needles and yarn in a way that is comfortable to them, with a bit of guidance about which techniques will work better than others, of course. I have, for the most part, ended up with knitters who happily knit in a number of different styles.

So, in the mid-1980s I was getting seriously passionate about knitting. I attended more TKGA conventions. I subscribed to every knitting magazine I could find. I ordered yarn color cards from vendors who advertised in these magazines. I got on vendor mailing lists and started getting catalogs. I bought new knitting books as soon as they were published.

I even did a bit of designing. I got out colored pencils and graph paper and designed several intarsia (designs created by using blocks of different colors to create patterns or motifs) sweaters that turned out surprisingly well, considering I had no idea what I was doing. I think naïveté and inexperience were to my advantage: I didn't know enough to be intimidated by the design process. There's a lot to be said for youthful enthusiasm and energy (not to mention ignorance). If something didn't work, I simply ripped it out and reworked it, often staying up all night to do so.

My knitting skills improved. I immersed myself in all things Fair Isle (designs consisting of horizontal bands of patterns knitted in no more than two colors in each row) for a while. Then I discovered British fisher ganseys (highly textured designs knitted at a fine gauge) and that was all I knitted for a couple of years. Then back to Arans for quite a few years. Then I discovered the joys of knitted lace, and my yearlong "lace period" ensued. And then I returned to Fair Isles.

I'm a bit more well-rounded in my knitting today. I switch back and forth between a variety of projects, often working on two or three different things in a day. I'll often have one relatively simple project on the needles to work on while commuting, one intensely complicated project to work on at home in solitude, and one simpler, but not completely mindless, project for winding down before going to sleep.

Nowadays, whenever I think about myself and who I am (which is admittedly not very often as I'm not too fond of introspection), "knitter" is the first word I use to describe myself. I think about knitting almost constantly. I dream about knitting. It is usually the last thing I think about before falling asleep and the first thing on my mind when I wake up in the morning. It is very rare that a day goes by when I have not knitted even a couple of rows. If I haven't knitted for a while, I find my hands going through the motions without the needles and yarn. And on the rare occasions when I complete a project and have nothing else on the needles, I feel anxious and unsettled until I cast on and start something new.

Knitting both revs me up and calms me down. Planning a new project, selecting the yarn, and getting started on it is a cause for celebration and excitement. When I'm selecting a project and the yarn that is just right for it, I feel as though I am giving myself a gift.

On September 11, 2001, I was trapped in the Washington, DC, subway system for most of the day, trying to get home. I was underground for hours, not knowing what was happening, or even what the world would look like when I finally got out of the subway. I knitted an entire sleeve of an Aran sweater that day, standing on the train platform at Metro Center with my skein of cream-colored wool yarn tucked under one arm. Working on my knitting, even though I was doing it numbly, on autopilot, was a great comfort. Doing something so familiar and ordinary, something that is a constant in my life, helped me get through the horror of that day. It has helped me get through many tough times.

I knit on the train going to work. I knit at my desk at lunchtime. I knit while reading, and while watching television. I knit while riding in (but not driving!) a car. I am always looking for ways to find more knitting time.

So, I present to you:

Top Ten Tips from the Wendy D. Johnson School of Letting Everything Else in Your Life Fall by the Wayside so You Can Squeeze in a Bit More Knitting Time

10. Get your hair cut in a style that requires no blow-drying or styling—that gives you an extra ten minutes of knitting time per day.

9. Have permanent eyeliner tattooed on—there are another couple of minutes saved.

8. Use paper plates and cups (preferably recycled) so you don't have to wash dishes. Better yet, live on bags of potato chips and pint containers of ice cream.

7. Take public transportation to work so you can knit during your commute.

6. When your clothes get dirty, buy new clothes so you don't have to waste time doing laundry.

5. When you buy new clothes, buy all black so you don't waste time coordinating your wardrobe. A bonus: everyone will think you're edgy and really cool.

4. Don't bother vacuuming your house. If pet hair builds up, just tell people you've adopted a furry decor.

3. Get caller ID so you don't have to waste time answering the phone unless it's Ed McMahon wanting to know where to deliver your check for a million dollars.

2. Encourage your significant other to take up a great new hobby—winding skeins of yarn into center-pull balls.

1. Learn to knit in your sleep!
   I knit, therefore I am.

Chapter 2 • The Laws of Knitting

"I COULD NEVER DO THAT. It looks so complicated."

That's often the first comment I hear from people who see me knitting. That, or "I could never do that. I don't have the patience."

At the risk of sounding incredibly contradictory, let me say that some knitting can be considered very complicated, while some knitting can be considered dead simple.

I have knitted items by following charts that barely fit on an 11-by-17-inch sheet of paper and at that size need a magnifying glass to decipher. And I have knitted items following patterns that are mindless. I have actually fallen asleep while knitting and upon awakening, found that I continued knitting while in a semiconscious or unconscious state. Knitting without errors, to my very great surprise. Now that's simple!

Knitting requires patience? Perhaps. But I am the world's most impatient person and I knit. A lot.

All knitting is essentially combinations of knit and purl and you build on those as you progress to cast on, bind off, increase, decrease, and finally, follow patterns.

But what are the laws of knitting? What must you do first? Are there rites of passage you must experience?

As far as I'm concerned, there are no laws of knitting! There you have it: my philosophy of knitting. The first law of knitting: there are no laws of knitting.

Yes, we knitters are a lawless bunch! We wield our needles recklessly, throwing caution and reason to the four winds.

There are some basic stages that most people go through, however. Everyone is different and will do things differently, but I know I went through some steps from my first awkward fumblings with yarn and needles to where I am today.

As I learned to knit, I moved from unstructured to structured: no shaping (scarves, afghans), little shaping (hats, shawls), more shaping (vests, sweaters). There was also a progression in the sophistication of stitches and stitch combinations and how I used them: simple knit/purl combinations like ribbings, more complex knit/purl textures, then cables or lace. And of course there was a progression of skills: from two-needle knitting to circular and four-needle socks or sleeves to color work to steek construction.

There were also stages involving the materials I used. When I first started knitting, I used my mother's leftover yarn. There was a stage when I bought cheap yarn because I was a poor student and couldn't afford anything nice, but I couldn't stop knitting. Then there was that period when I may have turned into a yarn snob and bought only expensive and fine yarns. Knitting became an expression of creativity and art.

The stages of what you knit are often a natural progression. In my case, the first stage was the garter stitch square. Cast on some stitches and knit every row. When I was a little kid, I was the queen of the knitted doll blanket. They were sad, lopsided, uneven doll blankets, but they were my own work and I was darn proud of them.

Then you need challenges and you start to knit cables, color work, fitted garments, lace. . . .

Different people take different approaches to knitting. Some become obsessed with the process, some do it as a relaxing pastime, and others do it as a creative outlet. Some knit simply for the end result: a garment, an afghan, et cetera.

Some make it their lifework.

I learned to knit as a small child, so my knitting progressed from doll blankets to other childish things. It was quite a while before I graduated to sweaters. An adult wishing to learn how to knit may not be interested in knitting doll blankets. But a plain old dishcloth makes a great (not to mention useful) first project.

Plain Old Dishcloth

Materials

Worsted-weight cotton yarn (one 50-gram skein will make a couple of cloths)
US size 8 (5mm) needles

Directions

Cast on 30 stitches. Knit every row until you have a square. Cast off and weave in ends.

There you have it. Ta-da! A dishcloth.

Do you want something more challenging? Go ahead and make a ribbed dishcloth.

Ribbed Dishcloth

Materials

Worsted-weight cotton yarn
US size 8 (5mm) needles

Directions

Cast on 30 stitches.

Knit 1 stitch, purl 1 stitch across the row. Repeat on every row until you have a square. Cast off and weave in ends.

And there you have a ribbed dishcloth. You can vary this slightly to make a seed stitch dishcloth. On the first row you'll knit 1, purl 1 across your 30 stitches. On the second row purl 1, knit 1 across.

Do you want some variations? Get thee to a stitch dictionary!

I love stitch dictionaries and I own a number of them. A stitch dictionary is a compilation of different stitch patterns: knit/purl textures, cables, lace, et cetera. They have a photo of a swatch of knitted fabric for each stitch pattern, along with instructions for knitting. They get extra points from me if the instructions are charted, but the ones with written-out directions only are still extraordinarily useful. I can sit down and flip through a stitch dictionary and come away with several great ideas for things I want to knit using different pattern stitches.

Dishcloths are a great way to try out new stitch patterns and experiment with new knitting techniques. A small square is not a big investment in time or money, so if you mess up your pattern horribly, you've not lost much.

Here's a fun little texture pattern incorporated into a dishcloth.

Box Stitch Dishcloth

Materials

Worsted-weight cotton yarn
US size 8 (5mm) needles

Directions

Cast on 30 stitches.

Row 1: K2, *p2, k2; repeat from * to end.

Row 2: P2, *k2, p2; repeat from * to end.

Row 3: Repeat row 2.

Row 4: Repeat row 1.

Repeat these 4 rows until you have a square. Cast off and weave in ends.

Dishcloths are best knitted in washable cotton. However, some people (and I'm raising my hand here) are not overly fond of knitting with cotton. Personally, I find it tough on my hands. Cotton does not have the elasticity of wool, so I find myself struggling with cotton when I knit patterns where I need to move stitches, like cables. And what you would use for a dishcloth, a plain, sturdy cotton, is particularly hard for me to knit without some hand pain.

So you can practice knitting squares in wool. What are you going to do with a number of wool squares? Make an afghan!

Years ago, a coworker gave me a booklet (published in the 1950s) that had belonged to her mother-in-law. It was a pattern for an afghan that was composed of ninety-nine squares: two each of forty-nine different stitch patterns, one knitted in a dark color and one in a lighter color; plus one square that had an initial worked in it using both colors. A third color was used to crochet around each of the squares before joining them together.

I made that afghan, in three shades of blue. I used a nice quality acrylic yarn that felt like wool, because I wanted the afghan to be machine-washable.

Okay, time for a confession. I did not crochet around the squares myself. At that point in time, my crochet skills left a lot to be desired. (Oh, who am I kidding? My crochet skills still leave a lot to be desired.) I was making the afghan as a wedding gift for my brother, and I preferred that it not look as though a three-year-old had done the crochet.

The coworker who gave me the pattern conveniently had a mom who was a whiz at crochet and she crocheted around each square for me, and I knitted a cabled scarf for her. A fair trade indeed. We were both happy with the outcome. I do so love the barter system!

Knitting this afghan was a great experience for me. At the time I made it, I was a fairly experienced knitter. But still, some of the squares incorporated patterns I had never seen before. Some of them I did not enjoy knitting, but as they were all about five inches square, I never had to spend too much time on each one. The finished afghan is pretty large, but I could whip out two to three squares per evening, depending on the complexity of the pattern stitch of each square. And I had the great good sense to start the project way in advance of the date I actually had to give the afghan as a gift, so I was able to knit it at a leisurely pace. There's nothing like the panic of a deadline to screw up your knitting karma. Having plenty of time, I knit at a leisurely pace that suited me and was able to enjoy the process of making many little patterned squares.

An afghan constructed of individual squares is a great way to practice different stitch patterns and, as an added bonus, make something nice in the process. Apart from honing your knitting skills, it's also a great way to try out different yarns or to use up odd balls. If you are making an afghan like this for a gift, you can figure out pretty easily how long it will take you to make it by timing how long it takes to knit a single square. Multiply that by the total number of squares, and then allow a couple of days for assembling the afghan. Then, add two weeks to the total amount of time to allow for any unanticipated problems along the way.

So. You've knitted squares. You are a master at knitting squares. How about knitting a rectangle? Knit a scarf! A scarf, in its simplest form, is nothing more than a very long rectangle.

This first scarf is knitted from a lovely, extremely bulky yarn on huge needles. The stitch pattern is fisherman's rib, which is a fun variation of regular ribbing. It can best be described as a fat fluffy ribbing.

Fisherman's Rib Scarf

Materials

2 skeins Blue Sky Alpaca Bulky Hand-Dyed (50% wool, 50% alpaca, bulky weight, 45yd/100g skein)
US size 17 (12mm) needles

Gauge

Approximately 2 sts to the inch in the pattern on size 17 needles (gauge is not important here; I'm only including it to give an idea of the bulkiness of the yarn, should you want to substitute a different yarn).

Using two skeins of the specified yarn knitted on size 17 needles will give you a scarf that is approximately 6" wide and 55" long.

Directions

Cast on 8 stitches.
Purl 1 row.
Row 1: *P1, k next st in the row below; repeat from * to end.
Row 2: *K in the st in the row below, p1; repeat from * to end.

Repeat rows 1 and 2 until the scarf is approximately 55" long, or until you have approximately two feet of yarn left. End with castoff in purl, and weave in the ends.

This simple scarf, knitted in a beautiful yarn, is a quick and easy gift for you or for someone else.

Feeling adventuresome? Try a slightly more challenging scarf. The Scallop Scarf is knitted in a not-quite-so-bulky yarn as the Fisherman's Rib Scarf, on not-quite-so-huge needles, and incorporates some simple lace stitches.

Scallop Scarf

Materials

2 skeins Karabella Puffy (100% merino wool, bulky weight, 54yd/100g skein)
US size 13 (9mm) needles

Gauge

2.5 sts to the inch in pattern on size 13 needles (the same gauge disclaimer as above applies here).

Using two skeins of the specified yarn knitted on size 13 needles will give you a scarf that is approximately 7" wide and 52" long.

Directions

Cast on 19 stitches.
Row 1 (right side): K3, sl 1, k1, psso, k9, k2tog, k3.
Row 2: K3, p to last 3 stitches, k3.
Row 3: K3, sl 1, k1, psso, k7, k2tog, k3.
Row 4: As row 2.
Row 5: K3, sl 1, k1, psso, yo, (k1, yo) 5 times, k2tog, k3.
Row 6: Knit.

Repeat these 6 rows until the scarf is approximately 52" long, or until you have approximately two feet of yarn left. Cast off, and weave in the ends.

Now that you've got the hang of knitting lace with yarn-overs, try the Trellis Lace Scarf. It's knitted in a yarn that's lighter still: a heavy worsted weight. I've used a lovely cashmere/silk blend that is a joy to knit.

Trellis Lace Scarf

Materials

2 skeins Trendsetter Kashmir (65% cashmere, 35% silk, heavy worsted weight, 110yd/50g skein)
US size 10 (6mm) needles

Gauge

4 sts to the inch in pattern on size 10 needles (you don't need the gauge disclaimer by now, do you?).

Using two skeins of the specified yarn knitted on size 10 needles will give you a scarf that is approximately 6" wide and 38" long.

Directions

Cast on 29 stitches.
Row 1 (RS): K4, (yo, sl 1, k2tog, psso, yo, k3) to last stitch, k1.
Row 2: Purl.

Row 3: K1, (yo, sl 1, k2tog, psso, yo, k3) to last 4 sts, yo, sl 1, k2tog, psso, yo, k1.

Row 4: Purl.

Work the 4 pattern rows until the scarf is approximately 38" long, or until you have approximately a yard of yarn left. Cast off in rib, and weave in the ends.

Those three scarves require very little finishing work. All you have to do is weave in the yarn ends when you're done. The next scarf, the Fir Cone Scarf, requires a bit of finishing: blocking (shaping the knitted garment to its finished dimensions and shape) and the application of fringe.

Fir Cone Scarf

Materials

2 skeins Jade Sapphire Mongolian Cashmere (100% cashmere, heavy worsted weight, 100yd/55g skein)

US size 10 (6mm) needles

Gauge

4 sts to the inch in pattern on size 10 needles.

Using two skeins of this yarn knitted on size 10 needles will give you a scarf that is approximately 5" wide and 60" long, not including fringe.

Directions

Cast on 23 stitches.

Knit 2 rows.

Rows 1, 3, 5, and 7: K2, yo, k3, sl 1, k2tog, psso, k3, yo, k1, yo, k3, sl 1, k2tog, psso, k3, yo, k2.

Row 2 and all even-numbered rows: Knit across.

Rows 9, 11, 13, and 15: K1, k2tog, k3, yo, k1, yo, k3, sl 1, k2tog, psso, k3, yo, k1, yo, k3, ssk, k1.

Row 16: Knit across.

Repeat these 16 rows until the scarf is about 60" long. Knit 2 rows, then bind off.

In its present state, the lace pattern is somewhat closed up, so it needs to be stretched out, or blocked, to reveal its full beauty. To block the scarf, soak it in lukewarm water to which you have added mild soap or shampoo. Let it soak for a few minutes. Gently rinse it in lukewarm water, and squeeze out as much water as possible without wringing it.

Now lay the scarf out on a flat surface. I usually block my knits on the floor, covering the carpet with a couple of bath towels. You can do this on a bed covered with towels as well.

Gently stretch the scarf to the final width and length. As you stretch it, you will see the lace pattern open up. Pin the scarf to the floor at intervals to keep it stretched out. I find T-pins to be most useful for this. You can block as gently or as aggressively as you like: the more you stretch it, the more the lace will open up. I blocked my scarf quite gently, but some people may prefer a more open, airy look to the lace.

After you have pinned out your lace, let it dry completely. Depending on the temperature and humidity, this can take as little as twenty-four hours, or up to several days.

I should note here that cats enjoy the blocking process very, very much. They like to lie on the piece being blocked, ensuring that some cat hair is incorporated into the final design. Most of the photos I have taken of my knitting being blocked feature a cat reclining seductively on the lace.

When the scarf has dried, unpin it and release it from its bondage. Now, to make a fringe: cut remaining yarn into approximately 11" lengths and divide in half. Use half of your yarn pieces to make the fringe on the cast-on end:

Put two strands together and fold in half. With crochet hook, draw center of strands through first stitch of cast-on edge of scarf, forming a loop. Pull ends of fringe through this loop. In this manner, make fringe evenly across the entire cast-on edge of scarf. Repeat the process for the bound-off edge of scarf. Trim the fringe to even it up, if necessary.

Now that you've knit a few scarves—and should be sufficiently sick of knitting squares and rectangles—it's time to knit a matching hat or two. This hat is knitted in the round on double-pointed needles, which is not nearly as scary as it sounds. In fact, this is a good first project for double-pointed needles, as it's knitted on needles large enough so that you don't feel like you are juggling toothpicks. The resulting hat fits an adult head. Because it's ribbed, it'll stretch to fit a variety of head sizes.

Do you want a child's hat? Follow the same pattern, but substitute a worsted-weight yarn and US size 8 (5mm) double-pointed needles.

Easy One-Skein Hat

Materials

1 skein Noro Transitions (55% wool, 10% silk, 7% cashmere, 7% angora, 7% alpaca, 7% kid mohair, 7% camel, bulky weight, 132yd/100g skein)
US size 10 (6mm) double-pointed needles

Gauge

3.5 sts to the inch on size 10 needles

Directions

Cast on 72 stitches on double-pointed needles, join, and, working in the round, work k3 p3 ribbing in the round for 10".

Shape top:

Next round: (K1, k2tog, p1, p2tog) to end of round—48 stitches.

Next round: (K2, p2) to end of round.

Next round: (K2tog, p2tog) to end of round—24 sts.

Next round: K2tog to end of round—12 sts.

Next round: K2tog to end of round—6 sts.

Cut the working yarn, leaving a couple of inches. Finish off by threading the yarn end through the 6 remaining stitches and pull tight. Secure the end of the yarn on the wrong side.

You can, if you have enough yarn left over, make a pompom and sew it on top of the hat. Cute, but not mandatory!

You are proficient in squares, in scarves, and in hats. It's time for a sweater: a nice easy one in bulky-weight yarn. It has simple shaping, but a fun lace border at the bottom and on the sleeves to keep you from being too bored.

I named this sweater "Vince" because the lace pattern I used for the borders is called vine lace. For some reason, I am incapable of typing the word "vine"—it always comes out as "vince" on the first try. So I've given up, and named the design Vince.

I knitted this sweater using my own handspun yarn, but the recommended yarn in the pattern knits exactly to the same gauge as my handspun.

Vince Sweater

Finished Measurements

37½ (42)" chest
23" length

Materials

7 (9) skeins Brown Sheep Lambs Pride Bulky (85% wool, 15% mohair, 125yd/113g skein)
US size 10 (6mm) needles

Gauge

12 sts and 16 rows = 4" measured over stockinette stitch on size 10 needles

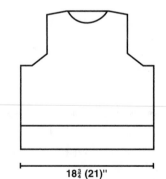

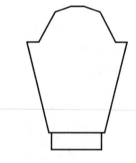

(23)"

18¾ (21)"

Vine Lace Chart

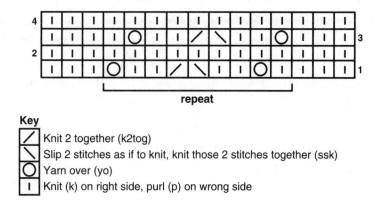

repeat

Key

╱	Knit 2 together (k2tog)
╲	Slip 2 stitches as if to knit, knit those 2 stitches together (ssk)
O	Yarn over (yo)
I	Knit (k) on right side, purl (p) on wrong side

Directions

Back

Cast on 59 (69) stitches.

Work Vine Lace pattern as follows for 16 rows:

Row 1: K3, *k1, yo, k2, ssk, k2tog, k2, yo; repeat from * to last 3 stitches, end k3.

Row 2: Purl across.

Row 3: K3, *yo, k2, ssk, k2tog, k2, yo, k1; repeat from * to last 3 stitches, end k3.

Row 4: Purl across.

On the next row, decrease 3 stitches evenly across—56 (66) stitches remain.

Continue in stockinette stitch until your work measures 15" from the bottom of the Vine Lace pattern.

Shape armholes:

Bind off 3 stitches at the beginning of the next 2 rows.

Bind off 2 stitches at the beginning of the next 2 rows.

Decrease 1 stitch at each end of every other row 4 times—38 (48) stitches remain.

Work straight until the armhole measures 9½" from the first bind-off.

Shape shoulders:

37½" size:

Bind off 4 stitches at the beginning of the next 6 rows.

Bind off remaining 14 stitches.

42" size:

Bind off 5 stitches at the beginning of the next 4 rows.

Bind off 4 stitches at the beginning of the next 2 rows.

Bind off remaining 20 stitches.

Front

Work as for the back until the armhole measures 8" from the first bind-off.

Shape neck:

Work across 14 (18) stitches, join a second ball of yarn and bind off the center 10 (12) stitches, work to the end of the row.

Working both sides at once, bind off 1 (2) stitch(es) at each neck edge once, and 1 stitch at each neck edge once (twice)—12 (14) stitches remain.

Work to match the back in length and shape shoulders as for the back.

Sleeves

Cast on 40 stitches.

Work Vine Lace pattern as follows for 16 rows:

Row 1: K3, *yo, k2, ssk, k2tog, k2, yo, k1; repeat from *, end k1.

Row 2: Purl across.

Row 3: K2, *yo, k2, ssk, k2tog, k2, yo, k1; repeat from *, end k2.

Row 4: Purl across.

Continue in stockinette stitch for 1", ending with the right side facing you.

Increase 1 stitch at each end of the next row, and each following 4th row for a total of 6 times—52 stitches.

Work until sleeve measures 18" from the bottom of the Vine Lace pattern.

Shape cap:

Bind off 3 stitches at the beginning of the next 2 rows.

Decrease 2 stitches at the beginning of the next 2 rows.

Decrease 1 stitch at each end of every 4th row 2 times.

Decrease 1 stitch at each end of every other row 8 times.

Bind off 3 stitches at the beginning of the next 2 rows.

Bind off the remaining 16 stitches.

Finishing

Sew front and back pieces together at shoulders. With a circular needle, starting at the right shoulder seam, pick up 3 stitches down the right back neck, 14 (20) stitches along the center back neck, 3 stitches up the left back neck, 18 stitches down the left front neck, 10 (12) stitches along the center front neck, and 18 stitches up the right front neck—66 (74) stitches.

Join and, working in the round, purl 1 round, then bind off knitwise on the next round.

Set sleeve caps into armholes, then sew sleeve and side seams.

Chapter 3 • "Virtuality" versus Reality

I WAS AN IMPASSIONED KNITTER long before widespread Internet availability.

In the beginning, I bought cheap yarn from craft stores and discount stores, with an occasional foray into a department store that sold yarn (and those are few and far between today, if indeed there are any left at all), and an even rarer trip to an actual yarn shop.

During the brief period of time that I worked in an actual yarn shop, I bought all my yarn there. I continued to buy yarn at that shop after I quit my job there.

When I discovered knitting magazines and, more important, the advertisements in the back of knitting magazines, I started mail-ordering yarn as well. I still went to a couple of local yarn shops though.

Once I had established firmly in my head that knitting was my number one all-consuming pastime (some might say obsession), I often found myself in a position where I could suck other people into knitting. This was most easily accomplished at work. I set up a lunchtime knitting group. A few of the people who attended already knew how to knit; the rest I taught. All of my victims were women, except for one man who showed up and gamely started a scarf. At the time I suspected that his motives were not pure and it turned out I was right. He just wanted to hang out with the chicks with sticks.

The knitting group was working out nicely. Those who weren't destined to be knitters quietly dropped out and slunk away, and those who were progressed in their skills. We met once a week and bonded over the needles. Coworkers who stopped by to mock and ridicule us were threatened with death by knitting needles. Sweaters were completed and cheered over, mistakes were made and corrected.

Spurred on by this positive experience with interactive knitting, I attended a meeting of a local knitting guild. What a disaster that was. I was the youngest person there, and by far the most experienced knitter. This did not sit well with the older regulars, who seemed put out by the sight of a younger person knitting a complex Fair Isle while they were working on far less intimidating designs. They made it clear to me that I was not welcome. I never went back after the first visit.

I changed jobs soon after that, so my lunchtime knitting group broke up. We attempted to get together one evening a month, but life got in the way, as it often does. One woman was a new mom with new demands on her time and another moved too far away to be able to easily attend, so our group disbanded.

I attempted to find knitters and knitter-wannabes at my new job with no luck. So it was back to my solitary knitting ways.

Then I discovered the Internet.

My first exposure to the online world was at a friend's office, as my place of employ did not yet have Internet access—very few did in the early 1990s. I had stopped by to pick up a friend after work and was offered the opportunity to check out the World Wide Web on his computer. The very first search term I entered into a search engine was "knitting." It returned a disappointingly small number of hits—a couple of bulletin boards and a sparse resource list or two.

In 1995 I bought a home computer and got Internet access. Less than a year later I got a cable modem connection, as I was fortunate enough to live in an area where it was being made available as a pilot program. That service provider offered space for its subscribers to set up a home page.

Being a quasi-geek, I of course had to set up a home page. I learned some basic HTML skills and bought a tiny scanner for an exorbitant amount of money. I took photos of my knitting (and my cats), scanned them, uploaded them, and made a home page.

It was ugly, I admit, but it wasn't as horrible as it could have been. I do have some artistic talent and design skills, as well as a background in publications layout. But it was pretty basic.

I updated my home page every time I completed a sweater, arduously taking photos, getting them developed, then scanning and uploading them.

Somewhere along the line, a couple of years later, I discovered an e-mail messaging list for knitters and happily subscribed. The Knitlist! This was a turning point. I had always been a somewhat solitary knitter, and suddenly I was in contact with hundreds (and later thousands as the list grew) of other knitters.

Some of these people posted a message every single day. Some of these messages were interesting and all about knitting. Some were not so interesting and not so much about knitting. I learned way more about someone's pregnancy and the birth of her son than I felt was necessary. But I also learned about others' attitudes toward knitting, what projects other people were working on, and what yarns they were using.

The most important concept I learned through the Knitlist was the Stash.

Up to this point I did not have a stash. When I was halfway through a project, I'd start planning my next project and buy the yarn for it, either via mail order or the local yarn shop. But I was now reading about people who kept yarn stashes. Some of them huge. The stashes, not the people. Though the people may have been, too. You never know.

At about the same time that I discovered the concept of stashing yarn, I discovered eBay. This was a very dangerous combination.

I will spare you the sordid details, and simply tell you that today I have an enviable stash. My guest room is filled with yarn. Yarn stuffed in bureaus, yarn stacked on shelves, yarn stored inside coolers. My linen closet houses even more yarn. There is a cabinet crammed full of sock yarn in my master bedroom. There is yarn in the wall unit in the living room, yarn on top of the microwave in the kitchen, yarn in hanging baskets, yarn in a gold wire cage on my coffee table. Yarn dangles seductively off a sofa table. A bouquet of hand-painted skeins of yarn rests in a pretty porcelain milk pitcher on my dining room table. There is an acronym that online knitters use: SABLE. It stands for Stash Acquisition Beyond Life Expectancy. They must have been talking about me.

While I know there is very little chance of sheep becoming extinct, I buy yarn as though they were on the endangered species list. Somewhere in the back of my head lurks the fear that someday I'll want a particular yarn, and it will no longer be available. I simply cannot risk that. Stashers will understand.

As the Internet grew in popularity, splinter e-mail lists formed. I joined an Aran knitting list, a lace knitting list, and formed my own Norwegian knitting list. More and more yarn vendors were opening up online shops, and the brick-and-mortar yarn shop where I had briefly worked closed. I reached a point where I purchased all my yarn online.

I bought my own domain name and set up a more sophisticated website. There were still some cat photos and "what I did on my vacation" content, but the main focus was knitting. I bought a digital camera and was suddenly able to post update photos of my work in progress far more easily than the old take-a-picture–get-it-developed–scan-it routine.

I started corresponding via e-mail with a few knitters who had written asking me questions about one thing or another. I still participated on e-mail lists. My knitting website became better known. All of my knitting interaction with others was done online.

In the spring of 2002 I was out of town at a training course for work that lasted two weeks. During that time I relied on my knitting lists and e-mails for entertainment in the off-hours more heavily than usual. Someone mentioned on a list that she had set up a knitting blog.

What's a blog? I wondered.

I did a little research and discovered that "blog" is short for "weblog"—an online journal. There are blogs about anything you can imagine—personal journals, blogs about politics, society, food, and cooking. And of course, there are blogs about knitting.

Of course I had to have a blog! I set one up on my website and joined the Knitting Blogs Web Ring.

A web ring is group of websites with a common theme, linked together in a loop, allowing users easy access to subsequent sites in the ring by clicking on the links that are displayed on every member site. The Knitting Blogs Web Ring, like most of them, has a set of rules that member blogs have to follow. Basically, a member blog's main focus has to be knitting and it has to be updated regularly.

During the first few months of the Knitting Blogs Web Ring there were only a handful of members. We installed commenting systems so that we could post comments on each other's blogs. We linked to each other's blogs. We talked about what our blog neighbors were knitting. We cheered each other on, celebrating knitting triumphs and sympathizing over knitting disasters. And a bit of each blogger's personality and life came through on her blog. Some bloggers posted photos of their children wearing their hand-knits, some bloggers (me included) posted pictures of their pets. We shared recipes and chitchat about life in general, and knitting in particular.

About six months after I started my blog, in a frenzy of geekiness, I bought another domain: wendyknits.net. I set up a fairly sophisticated online publishing system there that was designed specifically for blogs, and used that site exclusively for blogging.

The Knitting Blogs Web Ring continued to grow. We continued to read each other's blogs and comment. Some people discontinued their blogs, but many more people started new ones. We swapped yarn, participated in knit-alongs where everyone knitted the same pattern at the same time, and indulged in other knit-related activities, just like members of a local guild might.

Then something amazing happened.

My birthday is January 2. I have spent my entire life complaining to anyone who would listen that my birthday is often overlooked, forgotten in the post-holiday doldrums. In the autumn of 2002 I briefly whined about this online in another knitter's blog comments (where she was discussing birthdays) and forgot all about it.

On January 1, 2003, a wrapped gift appeared on my kitchen counter. When I asked my boyfriend, Ian, about it, he just shrugged and said, "I guess you should open it."

Inside was a knitting book that was on my wish list. It was from an online acquaintance—a knitter in Brazil. I was amazed. How did she know? I was so touched that she went to all the trouble and expense to have it sent to my boyfriend so that he could give it to me.

The next day, another gift mysteriously appeared. This time it was a skein of lovely sock yarn from another online knitting friend in Germany. The next day, another gift from another knitter. The next day, another.

I returned to work after the holidays. There was a gift waiting for me on my coworker Odie's desk. And one the next day.

By this time I figured out that there was a conspiracy going on and, not being completely brain-dead, I even vaguely remembered the online conversation about my January birthday.

I received a different gift from a different knitter from a different place in the world every single day that month. And cards and notes from most of them telling me the significance my knitting and my participation in the online knitting community had had for them. Some of these women I barely knew, and I was amazed. I am still amazed. Only one of these women had I ever met in person.

At the end of the month, the conspiracy was revealed to me, and I was given access to the online group that the organizers had set up to manage this surprise. I spent a wonderful couple of days reading the more than five hundred messages that the group members had exchanged over several months. The first ones discussed my likes and dislikes, what knitting books I may already have, and what they were going to give me for gifts. Later they discussed the mechanics of getting the gifts to my boyfriend and coworker for distribution, and the last messages were about my reactions to the gifts and the fun of seeing when I would figure out what was going on.

I am still touched, amazed, and humbled at this generous outpouring of knitting love and friendship. I was still knitting alone at this point, but was I a solitary knitter? Not on your life!

As a result of "WendyMonth" (as the organizers called it) I made some important real-life friendships. That summer I met several of the participants in Ontario, Canada, for a mini retreat at the vacation cottage of one of the knitters. It was all girls, all knitting, all the time, and the most fun I can remember having in a long time.

So I continued to blog about my knitting, posting updates and photos every weekday about what I was knitting. In an effort to keep my blog entertaining, I started a monthly contest, giving away something knitting-related in a drawing. (Having a huge yarn stash does have its benefits.)

My readership grew and grew. According to my website statistics, my blog was attracting a million visitors a month. Then two million. Then three million. Then four. I got masses of e-mail daily, some of it from people asking for help with their knitting, some of it simply fan mail.

I still don't completely understand why my knitting blog is so popular. I'm not the best or fastest knitter in the world, nor am I the best knitting writer. Some days it's an effort to find something to blog about. (Yes, we use "blog" as a verb.) But with very few exceptions, I do post an entry to my blog for every weekday, rain or shine. And I always try to post at least one photo. I think consistency of effort is a good thing.

In December 2003 I read on one of the knitting blogs I regularly visit, Digital Yarn, that the blogger, Kristine, was planning to open a yarn shop in the spring. To my surprise and delight, I realized that she was opening the shop in Alexandria, Virginia, my hometown. At this point I hadn't been in a local yarn shop in over five years, preferring to buy yarn online.

I met Kristine right after the holidays. We were both involved in an online yarn swap project (set up by yet another knit blogger) and we had arranged to meet over coffee to pass on the yarn swap box. After battling my initial response upon meeting her that I really ought to hate her because she was not only younger than I but gorgeous, I discovered that Kristine was a kindred spirit. She told me some of her plans for the shop: cozy little corners with comfy chairs to promote spontaneous knitting, a fun color scheme, classes it would offer, events it was planning, yarns it would be selling. It sounded like great fun! Even the name of the shop was fun: Knit Happens.

Kristine documented the birth of her yarn shop on her blog and I followed along in breathless anticipation. Every day she posted photos of the retail space being renovated and painted and the arrival of stock for the shop. I scheduled a day of leave from work during its first week of opening and arranged with a knitting friend from Richmond, Lindsey-Brooke (who I met online because of WendyMonth), to meet up and descend on Knit Happens.

My first visit to Knit Happens. What can I say? I felt like I was returning to the mother ship. Stepping inside the shop was like stepping into a little slice of fibery paradise. Kristine welcomed us warmly and we spent a long afternoon exploring every fiber-filled inch. Kristine refers to her shop as "Nirvana for Knitters" and it's certainly true!

I had been in many yarn shops before, but nothing like this one. The shop where I worked in the early 1980s was more of a yarn supermarket. It was a large retail space and very antiseptic, painted all off-white. The yarn was neatly arranged in little cubbyholes and the needles and other tools hung on a pegboard. Most of the other shops I had been in were cramped and messy with no space to sit and knit. And some of them were owned or managed by . . . well . . . cranky, opinionated curmudgeons who were less than welcoming.

Knit Happens is located in Alexandria's Old Town, a fashionable and historic district of the city. The shop is painted pink and green, and there is a large sunny bay window in the front of the shop, with comfortable, pretty armchairs and a coffee table arranged by the window. They even have man-friendly magazines set out for those who have been dragged into the shop by knitters. The walls are lined, of course, with cubbyhole bookcases filled with yarn, but there's so much more. There are baskets everywhere filled with yarn. Cute little notions and knickknacks in unexpected places. Pegs draped with skeins of glorious hand-painted yarns. Bookcases full of knitting patterns and books. And a large table and chairs in the back of the shop, providing a perfect place to hold classes, or just sit and knit. It's not a large space, yet I can spend hours there, wandering around, thumbing through pattern books, pulling out skeins of yarn, making piles of coordinated colors on the table. The shop screams, "Stay a while! Sit down and knit!"

After a few visits, I realized that having a real-life flesh-and-blood (well, brick-and-mortar) yarn shop to visit has changed my view of knitting. There's nothing like playing with different colors and textures to fire my enthusiasm and make the creative juices flow. I've put together complicated colorways and mixtures of textures for several fun projects. That's something you simply can't do in an online yarn shop, no matter how well their wares are photographed and displayed.

Here's an example of Wendy-epiphany. BKH (Before Knit Happens) I always chose very traditional designs to knit. Apart from that ongoing sock obsession I have, I knitted traditional Fair Isles, Arans, and Norwegian designs pretty much exclusively. These are beautiful, complicated designs that are a joy to knit and a joy to look at. Well, at least in my opinion they are. However, high fashion they are not. They are works of art but not always flattering apparel, usually being somewhat boxy in shape.

AKH (After Knit Happens) my thinking changed. Influenced by what's available in the shop and the people with whom I've come in contact there, I've branched out. I still love my traditional designs and always will. But I've made some lovely items that are far more haute couture and far more flattering to the female form. And I've designed some fun little sweaters, influenced by yarns I've found there.

I've learned that I don't always have to knit the most complicated design I can find (or dream up) on the tiniest needles possible. It's not a contest.

There's nothing wrong with knitting something fun and fashionable just because you want to.

Becoming a regular at Knit Happens (or one of the "Irregulars," as we call ourselves) is doing wonders for my stash, but is definitely making a dent in my pocketbook. It's hard to describe the thrill one gets from being there, on the spot, when Jimmy the UPS guy wheels in several huge boxes of new yarn on his hand truck.

How big an effect has having a local yarn shop had on my yarn consumption? Let's just say that if I wanted to wallpaper my living room with Knit Happens shopping bags, I'd have no problem covering all the walls. I could probably do the ceiling, too.

I was in the shop one day and saw that Kristine was offering some lovely fine 100% silk yarn for sale. This is truly a luxury yarn, something you would use to knit something very special. An idea for a design popped into my head: a tank top with a bit of body shaping and a dainty lace edging. Sadly, the yarn I used for this design is no longer available, but any fingering-weight yarn that meets the gauge requirements will work.

I present to you:

Lucky Tank Top

Finished Measurements

34 (38, 42)" chest
19 (19½, 20)" long

Materials

500 (600, 700) yards fingering-weight silk or cotton yarn

US size 2 (3mm) needles (or size to obtain gauge), and 16" circular needle one size smaller

Gauge

7 sts and 9 rows = 1" on size 2 needles

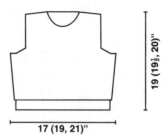

19 (19½, 20)"

17 (19, 21)"

Lace Pattern Chart

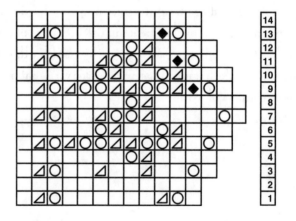

Key

☐	Knit (k)
◯	Yarn over (yo)
◆	Knit 3 together (k3tog)
◺	Knit 2 together (k2tog)

Lace Pattern in Words

Using size 2 needles, cast on 12 stitches.

Row 1: K1, yo, k2tog, k6, yo, k2tog, k1.

Row 2: Knit.

Row 3: K1, yo, k2, k2tog, yo, yo, k2tog, k2, yo, k2tog, k1.

Row 4: K7, yo, k2tog, k4.

Row 5: K1, yo, k1, k2tog, yo, yo, k2tog, k2tog, yo, yo, k2tog, yo, k2tog, k1.

Row 6: K5, yo, k2tog, k2, yo, k2tog, k3.

Row 7: K1, yo, k4, k2tog, yo, yo, k2tog, k2, yo, k2tog, k1.

Row 8: K7, yo, k2tog, k6.

Row 9: K1, yo, k3tog, k2tog, yo, yo, k2tog, k2tog, yo, yo, k2tog, yo, k2tog, k1.

Row 10: K5, yo, k2tog, k2, yo, k2tog, k3.

Row 11: K1, yo, k3tog, k1, k2tog, yo, yo, k2tog, k2, yo, k2tog, k1.

Row 12: K7, yo, k2tog, k4.

Row 13: K1, yo, k3tog, k6, yo, k2tog, k1.

Row 14: Knit.

Directions

Back

With size 2 needles, cast on 12 stitches and work 8 (9, 10) repeats of lace pattern. Bind off, but do not cut working yarn.

Using working yarn, pick up and knit 112 (126, 140) stitches along straight edge of pattern. Starting with a wrong side row, work 7 rows in the following pattern:

Wrong side: K1, *p12, k2; repeat from * to last stitch, end k1 instead of k2.

Right side: P1, *k12, p2; repeat from * to last stitch, end p1.

Working increases into the pattern, increase 1 stitch at each end of the next row, and then every 8th row 3 times—120 (134, 148) stitches.

Work in pattern until piece measures 10½ (11, 11½)".

Decrease 1 stitch at each end, every other row 5 (9, 12) times—96 (98, 102) stitches remain.

Continue in pattern until piece measures 18½ (19, 19½)" from the start.

Shape shoulders:

Bind off 7 stitches at the beginning of the next 4 rows.

Bind off 8 stitches at the beginning of the next 2 rows.

Bind off 52 (54, 58) back neck stitches.

Front

Work as for back, including all shaping, and, *at the same time,* when piece measures 15½ (16½, 16½)" begin neck shaping:

On next row, work 33 (34, 36) stitches, attach another ball of yarn, bind off center 30 stitches, and work across row. Working both sides at once, decrease 1 stitch at each neck edge, every other row 11 (12, 14) times.

Continue in pattern until piece measures 18½ (19, 19½)" from the start.

Shape armholes:

Bind off 7 (9, 11) stitches at beginning of next 2 rows.

Shape shoulders:

Work shoulder shaping (at shoulder edges) to correspond with back.

Finishing

Sew shoulder seams.

Work armhole edging:

With smaller size 16" circular needle, pick up 112 stitches around armhole edge. Work back and forth:

Knit 1 row (wrong side).

Knit 1 row (right side).

Knit 1 row (wrong side).

Bind off knitwise (right side).

Repeat for second armhole, then sew side seams.

Work neck edging:

With smaller size 16" circular needle, pick up 142 (144, 148) stitches around the neck edge. Join and work in the round:

Purl one round.

Knit one round.

Purl 1 round.

Bind off knitwise.

Weave in all ends and gently steam-press to block.

Chapter 4 • Knitting and Others

I SPENT A WHOLE LOT OF YEARS KNITTING SURREPTITIOUSLY, indulging only in private, almost as though it was a forbidden pleasure. I was even a little defensive about the whole idea of knitting.

I'm not exactly sure why I felt the need to keep my knitting to myself. While I didn't expend a whole lot of energy in an effort to keep my knitting secret, I also didn't go out of my way to show it to other people. I believe it's tied up in some way with self-perception and self-worth issues. While I have a pretty high opinion of myself and my abilities these days (rightly or wrongly), I didn't come out of the box that way.

I was a quiet and timid child and oh so painfully shy and antisocial. I remember that on the occasion of my third or fourth birthday party, my mother suggested that I sit in the middle of the floor and open my presents while all the guests looked on. The horror. I repeat, *the horror*. She had to physically push me onto the floor and as soon as she let go, I popped back up (did you ever have one of those toys that you could knock over, and it would bounce right back up again because the bottom was weighted?) and melted into the crowd. She finally gave up on that idea.

In retrospect, I wonder where my mother found a dozen or so children to actually attend my birthday party. Probably because she was (and is) a darn good cook and her cakes were (and are) to die for.

I was brought up in a time when children were supposed to be seen and not heard, respect their elders, et cetera. No doubt this had some influence on my personality, or lack thereof.

It was during my teen years that the women's liberation movement was really coming to the forefront. We, the already confused female adolescents, were getting the impression from all around us that we were supposed to es-chew the traditional womanly arts and values. We were supposed to strive to become high-powered career women. No knitting in the boardroom—that was a sign of feminine weakness.

I loved to knit, but, like any teenager, also wanted to be accepted by my peers, so I went underground with my knitting, only working on it in the pri-vacy and solitude of my room. I became a closet knitter.

The fear of public ridicule never stopped me from knitting over the years; it just kept me from flaunting it in public. Every so often I'd find another knit-ter at school or work, and would indulge in some rare lunchtime PDOK—Public Display of Knitting. And I went so far as to establish lunchtime knitting groups here and there along the way.

A few years ago I started to come out of the closet, so to speak, with my knitting. I decided it was about time I stopped feeling so self-conscious about knitting outside of the "knitting milieu." I started knitting at sporting events, social gatherings, conferences, parties, fire drills, and family dinners. I've knitted on planes, on trains, and in automobiles.

I get some funny looks sometimes from fellow commuters when I knit on the train. Most of the "regulars" ignore me, but I do get an endless string of comments prompted by my knitting. Young men tell me I remind them of their mothers or grandmothers who also knitted. So *not* what you want to hear from a cute twenty-something guy, right? Now and then someone will insist that I'm crocheting, not knitting, because I'm using one needle (a circular) instead of two straights. And I've gotten more than my fair share of people who look at me and exclaim, "Knit one, purl two?" and laugh hysterically at their own wit.

And then there are the comments on how much money I'm saving by knitting.

I was knitting on a sock one day during the morning commute, and a newbie got on and started watching, clearly fascinated. I was at the point where it was obvious that I was working on a sock—I just had a few more rounds left to do on the cuff. She struck up a conversation, asking how long it took me to knit a sock, who the sock was for, and so on. Then she said, in a confidential tone of voice, "That's really great! You must save a lot of money by knitting your own socks, don't you?"

Seeing the look on a total stranger's face when you tell her that each pair of hand-knit socks that you make costs between twelve and twenty dollars? Priceless.

And there are the information-sharers, those who want to be helpful.

I was on the train going home one day when an older man, obviously a tourist, sat next to me. He watched me knit for a while with rapt attention, and then started in on the conversation:

Him: There's a big knitting museum in the town where I live.

Me: Really? Where is that?

Him: Paducah, Kentucky.

Me: Are you sure it's a knitting museum? I've never heard of a knitting museum there, and I think I would have known about it.

Him: Oh, yeah. It's really big. They have a show every year and when that's going on you can't get a hotel room for miles around. You *have* to go there!

I did some research when I got home and discovered that there is a quilt museum in Paducah, Kentucky. And yes, they do have a show every year.

And finally there are the just-plain-scary encounters.

On the train one morning, more or less pleasantly enveloped in my usual morning fog (made foggier by virtue of it being Monday), I was blindly knitting on my current sock in progress.

A young man sat down next to me.

Him: What are you making?

Me: A sock.

Him: A baby sock?

Me: No, an adult sock.

Him: Oh, the reason I asked is because my girlfriend missed her period so I guess we're gonna have a baby it's due sometime next summer so I'm going to have a kid and I don't know what to do because I'm gonna have a kid and what would you do here if you were gonna have a kid are you sure that's not a baby sock?

Me *(to self)*: Why me?

And there was the occasion when I got on the train and sat in the seat in front of two young Swedish girls. When I pulled out my knitting, one of them said to the other, in Swedish, "Oh, look, she's knitting, just like an old lady." And they laughed in a superior manner.

I turned around and said, *"Jag tala svenska"* ("I speak Swedish" in Swedish).

The poor girls turned beet red and got off at the next stop. I actually felt bad for them. I'll wager, however, that they never made that mistake again.

But as I said, most of the time people on the train just ignore me.

I do have the occasional encounter elsewhere. I was sitting in my local yarn shop one day, just hanging out with the gang, happily knitting along, when a man and woman came in. The woman spent a few minutes telling us what an expert knitter she was. And then she told me I was knitting "wrong." In a not very pleasant tone of voice. She was unable or unwilling to tell me exactly what was wrong with my knitting, but she kept insisting I was doing it wrong. I finally turned my back on her and ignored her, rather than attack her with flailing needles, which is what I really wanted to do. I am proud of myself for not letting her upset me too much (apart from being annoyed by her incredible rudeness).

Occasionally someone who has seen me knitting will ask me to teach him or her to knit. I always respond to these requests with enthusiasm. I am being offered the opportunity to bring another knitter into the fold! Rather, to suck another unsuspecting body into this all-consuming obsession.

I love teaching an absolute beginner how to knit. I've been knitting for so long that I usually don't stop and think about what I'm doing, the process of knitting. Seeing it through the eyes of a beginner is very enlightening. Every movement with yarn and needles is brand new. I have to deconstruct what I'm doing to be able to properly explain it to someone else. For me, it's like having to stop and think about every motion I make when I walk. Not only does it give me a better appreciation of the process, but I often come away learning or relearning some aspect of how we knit.

It's also an incredible ego boost to have a skill, something that you are really good at, and to be able to pass that knowledge and skill on to other people. I am viewed as the teacher, the expert. As I stumble through life, wondering what the heck is going on most of the time, it's nice to be in the position of being the person who knows what she's doing for a change. This has served me in good stead in other aspects of life.

Another phenomenon of knitting in public is the many requests I get from people to knit something for them.

"Will you knit a sweater for me?" could be, perhaps, the most dreaded question in the English language. I get asked this question by total strangers.

Some will magnanimously offer to pay me. I remember one girl I barely knew saying to me (confident that I would jump all over the offer), "I'd be willing to go as high as twenty bucks."

I don't think I need to tell you how wrong this is. In so, so many ways.

While I know that many people will and do (and are perfectly happy doing so), I will never knit a sweater for money. Ever. Nothing sucks the fun out of something for me as much as turning it into work, something I am required to do, something I have a deadline for. Okay, if someone offered me a fabulous sum of money for a hand-knit I'd quickly change my tune. I have my price. (I'm thinking a few million bucks here, something along the lines of *Indecent Proposal*.) But that has yet to happen and I'm betting it never will.

Don't misunderstand me. I love to knit for other people. But it has to be my idea for it to be any fun. Knitting a sweater for another is a wonderful thing—it's an act of friendship, an act of love.

Plus, there's a bonus here. I consider knitting a gift for another person a perfect excuse to buy more yarn. I am almost never satisfied with what I have in my stash. I think to myself, "Well, it has to be exactly right because it's a gift, right? So, logically, I must buy the perfect yarn." (I am a master at rationalizing myself into further yarn purchases whenever possible.)

Then, there is a whole process I go through. The idea takes form. I've decided to knit a sweater for someone I deem sweater-worthy. What fiber will I use? Wool, alpaca, silk, cashmere? What color would the recipient like? So . . . what style of sweater shall I knit? A pullover, a cardigan, a vest?

I spend a lot of time making these early, important decisions. I think about it, I dream about it. I change my mind seventy or eighty times. And once the pattern is decided upon and the yarn purchased, I embark on the knitting with great enthusiasm.

I always feel a thrill with a new project, and the thrill of a new project that will become a gift is among the best of the thrills that knitting can offer. As I knit, I tend to think about the recipient of the sweater. I visualize the person receiving the sweater and his or her delight (I hope) with it. I don't think I am a particularly superstitious person, but I like to think that warm thoughts coupled with knitting create positive energy that is transferred to the hand-knit item. It may sound a little "New Agey" and touchy-feely, but there you have it. I try to work good karma into whatever I knit whenever I can. I also seem to work a lot of cat hair into whatever I knit as well, as my cat is almost always firmly planted in my lap while I knit, but that's another story.

Most of my knitted gifts to family are greeted with great enthusiasm. I have no doubt that my parents' friends are heartily sick and tired of hearing about my parents' oh so talented daughter and how she oh so cleverly knit the sweaters they are wearing.

I cringe when I think of some of the monstrosities that I've inflicted on my parents over the years that they have not only worn out in public, but have worn proudly. And not only have they worn them proudly, but they tell everyone who will listen that I made them. Fortunately, the knitted items they get from me these days are fit to be worn in public.

And my brother, Dave, loves the sweaters I've knit for him as well. Years ago, when I was a teenager, I knit a sweater and gave it to him as a holiday gift. It was in a simply hideous bright blue acrylic I bought at a dime store and was knitted in a cable and rib pattern. Not a bad-looking pattern, but incredibly ugly yarn makes for an incredibly ugly sweater. I am very fortunate in that my taste has improved since then. At least I think it has.

My brother still has that sweater. Thirty-odd years later.

It's got fuzzy balls and pulls and snags all over it. It's matted in places with cat hair where Dave's old tomcat used to sleep on it. But it's in surprisingly good shape with no unraveling or holes.

In the event of a nuclear holocaust we all ought to have bomb shelters knitted from dime-store acrylic yarn.

And believe it or not, not only does he still have it, but Dave still wears that sweater.

A few years ago, his wife went on a campaign to get rid of the sweater. It offended her delicate sensibilities, and I can't say that I blame her. I wouldn't want it in my home. Dave adamantly refused. "My sister knit this for me," he'd explain patiently to her every time she brought up the subject of disposing of the blue horror.

A few years ago I knit Dave another blue sweater. This one I knitted in a soft medium blue out of a nice-quality wool/acrylic blend, so it was still machine-washable and therefore practical. I did a Shaker stitch raglan pattern. It's a thing of simple beauty.

I presented it to him at Christmas and suggested that this new blue sweater could replace his old blue sweater. And my sister-in-law tried again to get him to throw away the blue horror. He still refuses, and he still wears it. It does my heart proud! I've knit him many sweaters since that first atrocity, but that one, I believe, is his favorite.

Not every knitted gift is received with such an enthusiastic response.

A long time ago I knitted a beautiful little smocked baby dress for a coworker who was also a fairly close friend who had just had a baby girl. I went to see her a week or so after the baby was born and presented her with the gift. She tore the wrapping off of it, glanced at it, and said, with a deadpan expression on her face, "Oh. Thank you." And she actually tossed it on the floor. *I was floored.* I didn't expect undying gratitude, but I thought she could have mustered a little more enthusiasm. The friendship dwindled a bit after that.

And then there was the individual (who shall remain anonymous) I presented with a lovely Shetland shawl one Christmas. Said recipient came up with the brilliant idea of using it as a furniture slipcover, and tucked it in tightly on an upholstered chair. Of course the yarn broke in many places from people sitting on it. Clueless Recipient actually had the nerve to return it to me with the request that I fix it. I took it and stuffed it in a cupboard. Needless to say, it is still stuffed in a cupboard unfixed and this person has not received any more hand-knitted gifts from me.

I guess the bottom line is that giving a handmade gift is, to put it elegantly, a crapshoot. Some people love the hand-knitted items and love that I took the time to make something for them. Some people wonder why I'm too cheap to buy them something.

So I've finally worked out that I don't have to knit gifts for everyone on my list. Just because you can, doesn't mean you should. Some people don't even wear sweaters. And, if you can believe it, some do not want a knitted slipcover for their bathroom tissue or a tea cozy in the shape of a sheep. I've learned to become a more thoughtful gifter and try to think of the giftee—does this person really want hand-knit socks or gloves or scarf or hand-knit anything? What are flattering styles and colors for the recipient?

Sometimes I succeed and sometimes I fail with my knitted gift-giving strategy. But I always try.

By far the most important lesson that knitting and others' perception of knitting has taught me over the years is to stop apologizing, stop feeling defensive, and stop doing things simply because I think they are what is expected of me. This can certainly apply to life in general, and I apply it to knitting in particular.

I have spent too many years being defensive about knitting. Because I'm slightly neurotic (and some people might argue about my use of the word "slightly") I tend to worry about what other people think of me. The "old me" thought that everything I did had to be perfect, or at least appear perfect to other people. I had to finish what I started. I had to knit complicated patterns. I was, after all, an experienced knitter. After I "outed" my knitting by posting regularly on a website and then on my blog, these rules I set for myself became even more important.

But I recently had several epiphanies about my knitting. I realized that the type of stuff I've been knitting for the past ten years or so is not necessarily the type of stuff I want to wear.

I've spent years knitting very traditional stuff—Fair Isles, Arans, Norwegian designs. I love them and I love knitting them. But I have a cedar chest and a closet full of them and don't wear them very often. Most of the time it's too warm indoors to wear heavily textured wool knits or stranded color designs. And because I have a full-time job in an office, that's where my sweaters get worn most of the time.

Perhaps I should just hang them on the wall and call them art.

This is a corollary of the "just because you can, doesn't mean you should" idea. I was knitting these types of things because I was able to do so, and felt like I ought to be knitting the most complex things I could.

I took a hiatus from knitting complicated traditional designs and started knitting some fun, more fashionable things. This is due in large part to the influence of other people.

I read other knitting blogs and see what people are making. Why shouldn't I make a simple little cardigan? It would be perfect for office wear. I've joined knit-alongs and knitted the same design along with other knitters who vary from absolute beginners to seasoned veterans. I think we all gain from the experience.

I will never abandon traditional knitting. I will return to these classics from time to time. But I have broadened my knitting horizon. Knitting is supposed to be fun. Make it fun.

In the spirit of making knitting fun, I came up with what I affectionately call "The Bad-Ass Knitters' Manifesto" and published it on my blog. It was an instant hit, and embraced by knitters everywhere.

Of course, I got some criticism too, but the positive response greatly outweighed the negative. So, in the spirit of enabling knitters everywhere to "take back" the knitting, I present to you:

How to Be a Bad-Ass Knitter

1. Knit whatever the hell you want . . . whenever you want.
2. Buy as much yarn (and books and needles, et cetera) as you want, whenever the hell you want.
3. Never, ever apologize for knitting.
4. Never, ever apologize because you think something you knit isn't "good" enough.
5. Never, ever apologize about how you knit: right-handed, left-handed, or with your toes!
6. Traditional knitting is timeless.
7. Display your stash with pride!
8. You don't have to follow a pattern exactly—make changes if you wanna.
9. Never apologize for knitting cat or dog hair into your sweater. It's all the warmer!
10. Whenever a non-knitter asks you a stupid question, remember that you carry long, sharp sticks.

Of course, as a cat lover, I couldn't resist this, either:

Bad-Ass Knitters' Kitties' Manifesto

1. Sleep on whatever the hell you want . . . whenever you want.
2. Play with as much yarn as you want, whenever the hell you want.

3. Never, ever apologize for sleeping on knitting.
4. Never, ever apologize because you think your playing with yarn isn't "good" enough.
5. Never, ever apologize about how you tangle yarn: with your left paw, your right paw, or with your teeth!
6. Sleeping on traditional knitting is timeless.
7. Barf on your owner's stash with pride!
8. You don't have to tangle yarn exactly like other kitties do— make changes if you wanna.
9. Never apologize for your fur working its way into the knitting. It's all the warmer!
10. Whenever a knitter tries to remove you from his or her knitting, remember that you have sharp, pointy claws.

Since I have embraced the idea of knitting what pleases me, not what I think I should, I designed a little short-sleeved ribbed raglan pullover, in celebration of all the knitters who have influenced me and challenged me to knit outside my narrow, traditional box—the Lisa Ribbed Pullover.

Lisa Ribbed Pullover

Finished Measurements

34 (36, 38)" chest
20½ (21, 21½)" length

Materials

7 (7, 8) skeins Koigu Kersti (100% merino wool, 114yd/50g skein)

skein) US size 7 (4½ mm) needles (or size to obtain gauge) and 16" circular needle one size smaller

Gauge

21 sts and 30 rows = 4" in stockinette stitch on size 7 needles

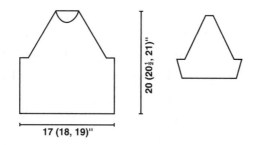

17 (18, 19)"

20 (20½, 21)"

Directions

Back

With the straight needles, cast on 90 (102, 114) sts. Work in pattern stitch as follows:

Row 1: *K2, p2; repeat from * across, end k2.

Row 2: *P2, k2; repeat from * across, end p2.

Work these 2 rows until piece measures 12½ (13, 13½)".

Start raglan shaping:

Note: For raglan decreases, work 2 stitches, decrease 1 stitch, work to the last 4 stitches, decrease 1 stitch, work last 2 stitches. Work the decreases according to their position on the piece:

Left-slanting knit decrease: knit 2 together through back loops

Right-slanting knit decrease: knit 2 together

Left-slanting purl decrease: purl 2 together through back loops

Right-slanting purl decrease: purl 2 together

34" size:

Bind off 8 stitches at the beginning of the next 2 rows.

Decrease 1 stitch at each end, every 3rd row, 13 times. [39 rows]

Decrease 1 stitch at each end, every 2nd row, 9 times. [18 rows]

Bind off remaining 30 stitches.

36" size:

Bind off 8 stitches at the beginning of the next 2 rows.

Decrease 1 stitch at each end, every 3rd row, 10 times. [30 rows]

Decrease 1 stitch at each end, every 2nd row, 10 times. [20 rows]

Work 1 row even.

Decrease 1 stitch at each end, every row, 8 times. [8 rows]

Bind off remaining 30 stitches.

38" size:

Bind off 8 stitches at the beginning of the next 2 rows.

Decrease 1 stitch at each end, every 2nd row, 24 times. [48 rows]

Decrease 1 stitch at each end, every row, 10 times. [10 rows]

Work 2 rows even.

Bind off remaining 30 stitches.

Front

Work as for back, including all shaping, until piece measures 20".

Begin neck shaping:

Work to center 18 stitches, attach another ball of yarn, bind off center 18 stitches, and work across row. Working both sides at once, decrease 1 stitch at each neck edge, every other row, 5 times.

Continue shaping as for back.

Bind off remaining 2 stitches for each side.

Sleeves

With the straight needles, cast on 74 stitches. Work in pattern stitch until piece measures 4".

Start raglan shaping:

Bind off 8 stitches at the beginning of the next 2 rows.

Decrease 1 stitch at each end, every 3rd row, 10 times. [30 rows]

Decrease 1 stitch at each end, every 2nd row, 11 times. [22 rows]

Decrease 1 stitch at each end, every row, 5 times. [5 rows]

Bind off remaining 6 stitches.

Finishing

Sew sleeves to front and back.

Make the neckband:

With the circular needle, pick up 100 sts around neck edge. Work in the round as follows: knit 1 round, purl 1 round, knit 1 round. Bind off loosely purlwise.

Sew up side seams and sleeves.

Chapter 5 • Knitting for Charity

I LOVE ANIMALS IN GENERAL AND CATS IN PARTICULAR. I have been besotted with cats for as long as I can remember. One of the earliest photos I have of myself is as a very young child—less than a year old—and in it I am crawling toward a black and white kitten that has a look of mild alarm on its face. I've been crawling toward cats and kittens ever since.

I've lived with cats my entire life, apart from a brief period in early childhood, so early that I can barely remember it, when my family owned a dog. And at one point as an adult, I had five cats at one time living with me. A bit excessive for a two-bedroom condominium, I admit, but I'm a sucker for a little kitty hard-luck story. All of these little guys were castoffs from uncaring humans. And I've never met a cat I didn't like, ever.

Eventually, as that herd of five cats died one by one in peaceful old age, I ended up with one cat, Isolde, nicknamed Izzy. She was a chubby little tabby with a snotty disposition and beautiful expressive green eyes. She and I co-existed peacefully, as long as my behavior met her minimum standards. She, in turn, did not mess with my knitting any more than she felt was necessary.

After I started my knitting blog, I was taking more and more photos of my knitting in progress, as I felt the need to have something new on the blog every day. One day I draped my knitting, a complex Fair Isle design, on the couch and left the room to get my digital camera. When I came back, Izzy was snuggled down on my knitting, a look of innocent contentment on her face. What a photo op! When I pointed the camera at her, she gazed into the lens with a soulful expression on her face. I took the photo and posted it on my blog. A star was born!

Knitters seem to be, for the most part, animal lovers, and everyone loved Izzy. I started posting photos of her every day. Izzy posing with a new yarn acquisition. Izzy reclining seductively on my work in progress. Izzy showing off a finished sweater. She was a natural: whenever I pointed the camera at her she'd gaze directly at it and hold still. I had my own spokesmodel!

But Izzy was an elderly cat, and at the age of seventeen, she became ill. I made the difficult decision to have her euthanized, rather than put her through a long and painful illness that would ultimately prove fatal, according to her veterinarian. I was, of course, devastated, as she'd been my faithful companion and harshest critic for years. I sadly reported her death on my blog, because she had many fans there who were concerned for her health and well-being.

I received hundreds of e-mails of condolence. Some knitters posted tributes to Izzy on other knitting blogs, and some made donations to the ASPCA and the Humane Society in her name. A couple even sent me cards and flowers. All of which provided a good measure of comfort.

I immediately started looking for another cat. Grieving period be damned! My home was too empty without a cat. Through the online service Petfinder, I found a local listing for a lovely two-year-old longhair cat with seal point Siamese markings and beautiful blue eyes. The exotic, elegant Lucy. The photo of her on the Petfinder site looked like a mug shot. In it her blue eyes were slightly crossed, giving her a look of alarm. My heart went out to her.

Lucy's owners had had her declawed, but let her go outside. She was attacked by dogs and, unable to defend herself, she was badly mauled. Her owners did not want to pay for medical attention for her, so they'd had a friend drop her at an animal shelter, claiming he had found her by the side of the road.

The shelter contacted an animal rescue organization, Capital Animal Care in Arlington, Virginia, to see if they could take Lucy and get her the medical attention she needed. Capital Animal Care took her in, paid for her medical treatment, and listed her with Petfinder to find a permanent home for her.

I contacted Lucy's foster mother, Barbara (who is also the director of Capital Animal Care), and we arranged for me to see Lucy at an adoption fair at a local pet shop. It was love at first sight, at least for me. Even though she was in a cage in a strange place, surrounded by strange animals and people, Lucy shoved her head under my hand to be petted when I extended my hand to her, and snuggled up against me when I picked her up.

Eight days later, quite appropriately on Mother's Day, Lucy came to live with me.

Lucy's photo made its debut on my knitting blog the next day and she was warmly welcomed by the members of the online knitting community who stop by my blog.

During the time that Lucy's adoption was pending, I had a dinner out with two visiting knitters. I told them about Lucy and one of them exclaimed, "Oh, Wendy! You have to host a catnip mouse knit-along when you adopt her!"

I thought this was a fun idea, so I suggested it on my blog. The idea was met with great enthusiasm, so I wrote up a pattern for a knitted mouse that had a simple cable running down the back and posted it online. A knitter in Norway made a cute little "Mouse-Along" graphic button that participants could post on their blogs if they wanted.

I encouraged people to send photos of their cats posing with completed mice and posted them online in a "Mouse-Along Photo Gallery" on my website. The project was a great success and all participants seemed to enjoy it immensely.

A month after Lucy came to live with me, her former foster mom, Barbara, stopped by for a visit. She saw Lucy's hand-knitted catnip mice and was charmed by them. Barbara worked part-time in a local pet shop and offered to sell mice for me if I wanted to make them, saying that she knew people would snap them right up.

I said thanks but instead of making mice for profit, why not make a few to donate to the rescue organization? Barbara was delighted with the idea. She made arrangements to sell the mice on behalf of Capital Animal Care through a local pet supply store that generously agreed to sell them without taking any profit.

Then I got to thinking—always a dangerous proposition for me. How many mice could I possibly make? Why not get other people involved? I didn't think I could reasonably expect people to knit catnip mice for my charity just because I asked them to, so I came up with the idea of a raffle.

I decided I would offer as a prize a kit to make a Norwegian sweater. (Once again, the obscenely large stash proved handy.) For every mouse knitted, the knitter would get one entry in the raffle. I posted this idea on my blog to see what everyone thought.

Wow! The response I got was amazing! Everyone seemed to think it was a great idea. Within an hour of my posting the idea, a lovely knitter and fellow cat lover e-mailed me and offered another sweater kit as a second raffle prize. When I received her donation in the mail, she had included a second kit to be used as yet another, third prize.

When everything was set up and organized, I had a total of seven sweater kits as raffle prizes—all donations by fellow knitters. Some people in other countries were not able to find catnip, or were concerned about customs regulations for sending catnip overseas, so two women in the United States volunteered as mouse-stuffers. The mouse-stuffers received empty mice from other countries, stuffed them with catnip, and sent them on to me. A couple of people wrote alternate mouse patterns, and my pattern was translated into Japanese and German. A couple of knitters in Germany and Japan acted as "mouse clearinghouses" in their countries, collecting mice from other knitters and sending them on to me.

And then the mice started pouring in. I posted updates every day on my blog and a running total of mice received. Some people sent cards and notes and little gifts for Lucy along with their mice.

I began to imagine that poor Lucy was starting to get a nervous twitch from being in the same place as all these mice and not being allowed to play with them. I shut all mice received in the guest bedroom and I did notice that she spent most of her spare time (when not eating, sleeping, or being spoiled by me) guarding the guest bedroom door.

By the time I had several hundred mice, I figured that it was time to start thinking about some kind of attractive packaging to help the mice sell. I did some online research and ordered a case of mouse-sized plastic Ziploc bags and sheets of blank adhesive labels. I designed a label, pressing Lucy into service for this endeavor. I posed her with one of her own hand-knitted mice and we had a photo shoot. The resulting label featured Lucy reclining with a blue mouse (to match her pretty eyes) and contained some brilliant ad copy describing the virtues of the hand-knitted catnip mouse. Plus, of course, a product endorsement by Lucy.

One night a week Ian and I sat down and labeled and stuffed mouse bags. Poor Lucy would sit in front of us, her little head whipping back and forth as the mice went from bin to mouse bag. She was vying for sympathy, but we did point out to her that it is difficult to look needy when one's own abundant catnip toys (including a mouse knitted from cashmere) are lying on the floor, abandoned.

The pet shop where Barbara worked very kindly volunteered to sell the mice without taking a cut of the proceeds, therefore, Capital Animal Care would receive all the money from the sales. On Saturdays we carted shopping bags of filled mouse bags over to the pet shop. One day when we were there, we saw a woman buy five mice, and several others get into a friendly fighting frenzy over the mice available.

All told, we received over fifteen hundred mice in the Great Charity Mouse-a-thon from knitters all around the world. Some people who had participated wrote to tell me that they were now knitting mice for their local animal charities, so the project was a huge success.

A catnip mouse is dead simple to knit, and it's fast and fun. It makes a great project for kids to work on, and knitting mice for your local animal shelter or rescue organization is a great way to start your children thinking about charitable contributions.

Here are two catnip mouse patterns to start you off. First, here is the excruciatingly easy one for beginner knitters.

Excruciatingly Easy Garter Stitch Catnip Mouse

Materials

A small amount of worsted-weight wool
Needles a couple of sizes smaller than you usually use for worsted wool
A tapestry needle
Catnip for stuffing

Directions

Cast on 30 stitches.

Knit 6 rows.

Next row: Knit 2 together, knit to end of row.

Repeat this row until you have 4 stitches remaining.

Bind off all stitches and leave a long tail of yarn for sewing up.

Fold the mouse in half lengthwise with the right side inside and sew the long seam along the bottom, leaving the back (the cast-on edge) open.

Turn right-side out and stuff firmly with catnip (your cat will probably enjoy helping you with this). From the right side, neatly sew the back cast-on edge together to close up the mouse. You can attach a couple more strands of yarn and braid them to make a tail, or you could make an I-cord tail if you're feeling intrepid!

How to make an I-cord:

Cast on 2 or 3 stitches onto a double-pointed needle. Knit across the stitches, then slide the work to the other end of the needle. Do not turn the work, but knit the stitches again, pulling the yarn over from the other end of the work. Continue on in this manner, sliding the work to the opposite end of the needle after each row, until you have the desired length.

Next, a slightly more difficult mouse—this is a great project piece for someone who would like to learn how to make cables but would like to work a small practice piece before embarking on a sweater.

Sophisticated Cabled Catnip Mouse
for the Debonair Cat-about-Town

Materials

A small amount worsted-weight wool

Needles a couple of sizes smaller than you usually use for worsted wool

A cable needle

A tapestry needle

Catnip for stuffing

Directions

Cast on 30 stitches.

Row 1: (K1, p1) 5 times, p2, k6, p2, (p1, k1) 5 times.

Row 2: (K1, p1) 5 times, k2, p6, k2, (p1, k1) 5 times.

Row 3: (K1, p1) 5 times, p2, (slip the next 3 stitches onto cable needle and hold behind work; knit the next 3 stitches from the left-hand needle, then knit the 3 stitches from the cable needle), p2, (p1, k1) 5 times.

Row 4: As row 2.

Row 5: P2tog, (k1, p1) 4 times, p2, k6, p2, (p1, k1) 5 times.

Row 6: P2tog, (k1, p1) 4 times, k2, p6, k2, (p1, k1) 5 times.

Continue in this manner, repeating the 6 rows for the cable pattern, and at the same time decreasing 1 stitch at the beginning of each row (as is shown for rows 5 and 6), and doing the cable twist on the 3rd row of the pattern until you have the last 10 stitches remaining, ready to work a right side row.

Next row: P2tog, k6, p2.

Next row: K2tog, p6, k1.

On the following row, bind off all stitches and decrease 2 stitches over the cable as you bind off (k2tog twice over the cable as you are binding off). Leave a long tail of yarn for sewing up.

Finish the mouse in the same manner as the Excruciatingly Easy Mouse.

On either version, you could add embellishments, like ears worked as bobbles, or you could use several different yarns in a single mouse. The variations are limited only by your imagination and yarn stash!

Spurred on by the success of the Great Charity Mouse-a-thon, I was ready for another charity project within a few months. I found out that an online friend, Liz Maryland Hiraldo, a talented designer in New York City, was designing a website for the Critter Knitters Coalition, an organization founded to provide comfort to homeless animals by distributing blankets (knitted, crocheted, sewn) to animal shelters. This seemed like just the thing for my next charity project, so I e-mailed Liz and asked her if she'd be interested in cohosting a charity blanket-knitting event with me. I suggested a similar format to the Mouse-a-thon, with prizes to be raffled. An animal lover herself, she immediately agreed, and generously dug deep into her stash for some prizes.

I contributed some prizes as well, and Liz and I were busy for the next couple of weeks working out the details. We set up web pages for the Critter Knitters Knit-a-thon, describing the project, the requirements for the blankets (size, washability, et cetera), links to patterns, raffle tickets, and photos of the prizes.

As soon as we announced the project, people started donating prizes. Wonderful prizes! We received beautiful yarn, knitting books, and other knitting-related items. One woman even donated a "woolly board," a device used for blocking traditional Fair Isle sweaters. We ended up with over seventy prizes.

I was designated as "Prize Central" and received all donations, photographed and posted them on the prize page, and then mailed them out to the winners at the end of the project.

Liz organized several Sunday afternoon "Knitting in the Park for Critters" events, where people could show up, hang out, get started on a blanket, and socialize. We put together some instant prize packages specifically for these events, and Liz held a drawing at each one and gave a prize away.

In the five months that the project ran, we received over sixteen hundred blankets. Liz photographed all blankets received and posted the photos online. The sight of these blankets could melt the hardest heart. They are all beautiful, and knitted with love. Some cat-sized, some puppy-sized, and some dog-sized. Some knitted, some crocheted, and some quilted. And as far as I'm concerned, each one is a work of art.

Knitting a critter blanket to be used by an animal shelter or rescue organization is simple. First, pick a yarn that is machine-washable. Using the needle size recommended for the yarn, cast on as many stitches as you need to make the blanket as wide as you want it to be. Then just knit. Knit until it's the size you want, or until you run out of yarn!

Knitting a critter blanket is a great way to try out stitch patterns, too. It's small enough so you won't get too bored before you finish it, but large enough to really show a pattern to advantage. Consider it a really big gauge swatch!

My most recent "knitting for charity" project was for Petfinder. I have a design for a knitted and felted kitty bed (which can work for small dogs, too) that I offered free on my website. I made two of them for Lucy and posted photos of her in her beds. Other people started using my pattern and sent me photos of their cats relaxing in their hand-knit beds. I set up a "Kitty Bed Photo Gallery" on my website, much like the "Mouse-Along Photo Gallery," and posted these photos.

One morning in September 2004 I got an e-mail from the outreach coordinator at Petfinder. She had stumbled across my website, and the photos of the kitty beds. In her e-mail she said that November is Petfinder's Adopt a Senior Pet Month, when they encourage people not to forget older homeless pets when looking for a new friend to adopt. She wondered if she could get some handmade pet beds for any senior pets adopted via Petfinder in November.

I posted the idea on my blog and suggested we could have a project similar to the Mouse-a-thon and the Critter Knitters Knit-a-thon. Once again, there was lots of enthusiasm for the idea. I set up an online group for the pet bed knitters and offered a couple of prizes for the raffle. Several generous people offered further prizes. Several of us volunteered to felt pet beds for knitters who did not have the type of laundry facilities appropriate for felting.

When the project was finished, we sent over one hundred beds to Petfinder. Once again, people took the initiative to make more beds for their local animal charities.

What did I learn from these projects? Adopting a cat from a rescue organization opened my eyes to the plight of these types of organizations—operating on a shoestring, staffed by caring people who sacrifice time and money to help animals in need. And being part of a community of caring people—the online knitting community—we have been able to do a little to help these wonderful people. Long may it continue!

As a result of the pet bed project, I refined and improved my pattern and am presenting the improved version here. This version has sides that are

knitted to twice the desired height, then folded over and sewn down to the inside before felting. The thicker sides help the bed maintain its shape. It's fairly easy and lots of fun to make, and is a great way to use up bits of leftover wool yarn. You can alter the pattern fairly easily to make a bed for a larger pet. And it's perfect to sell at fund-raisers for your favorite animal charity. I always give blanket permission to anyone who wants to use my pet bed pattern to make beds to help a charitable institution.

Felted Pet Bed

Materials

Approximately 800 yards of heavy-weight wool (be sure it is not labeled superwash—it must be able to shrink in the washing machine)

Approximately 400 yards of mohair

Eyelash yarn (optional, for trim)

US size 15 (10mm) or larger double-pointed needles and 24" circular needle

Gauge

Approximate gauge before felting: 2.5 sts and 4 rows = 1" (the gauge is not really important; just make sure that you are using a needle large enough so that your knitted fabric is loose).

Please note too that the yarn amount can vary. For my sample bed, I started out using two strands of Manos heavy worsted-weight yarn held together with one strand of Colinette mohair. When I ran out of the Manos wool that I had, I subbed one strand of Colinette DK wool plus Colinette Graffiti along with the mohair, and achieved the same gauge. For the eyelash yarn I used one skein of Crystal Palace Splash.

You can use three strands of worsted-weight wool plus mohair, or a combination of worsted and bulky wool. You can use all one color, or several different colors for a striped effect. You can make the bed a bit larger or a bit smaller than the pattern directs. You are only limited by your imagination—and your yarn stash, of course.

Directions

With all of the yarns you are using except the eyelash held together, cast on 9 stitches on double-pointed needles.

Knit 1 round.

Knit 1 round, increasing by knitting into the front and back of each stitch—18 stitches.

Knit 3 rounds.

Knit 1 round, increasing by knitting into the front and back of each stitch—36 stitches.

Knit 6 rounds.

Knit 1 round, increasing by knitting into the front and back of each stitch—72 stitches.

Knit 12 rounds.

Knit 1 round, increasing by knitting into the front and back of each stitch—144 stitches.

You can switch to your circular needle at this point.

Knit 20 rounds (or enough to get the pre-felted diameter you want).

Next round: (Knit 10, k2tog) 12 times.

Knit 9 rounds without shaping.

Next round: (Knit 9, k2tog) 12 times.

Knit 5 additional rounds holding one strand of eyelash yarn together with the other yarns.

Knit 1 round using all the yarns except the eyelash, but do not cut the eyelash yarn.

Knit 5 rounds holding one strand of eyelash yarn together with the other yarns.

Next round: (Knit 10, make 1) 12 times.

Knit 9 rounds straight.

Cast off and cut all yarns.

Weave in the yarn ends. You now have what looks like a large loosely knitted bag. With the right side facing you, fold down the cast-off edge to the inside of the bed so that the one plain round that you knitted in between

the sections of eyelash yarn is at the top; in this way you create a double-thickness wall. Loosely sew the cast-off edge to the inside of the bed, using one of the wool yarns you used for knitting. You should attach it approximately where you decreased stitches to start working up the sides of the bed.

Felt the bed by placing it in a zippered pillowcase cover and washing it in the washing machine on a hot wash/cold rinse cycle with a bath towel or a pair of jeans in the washer for added friction, until it reaches the finished size you want. It usually takes at least two trips through the washing machine, but different machines vary, of course.

Now you need to block it. Stretch the now damp bed over something circular that's the right size. You can use a stockpot, a small trash receptacle, a plastic cake carrier, et cetera. If you don't have anything large enough in diameter, you can fold up a bath towel and tape it around your round object. Leave the bed on the blocking form until it's completely dry.

Once the bed is dry, pop it off the blocking form and present it to your favorite feline or canine!

Chapter 6 • Why a Sock?

WHY ON EARTH WOULD ANYONE BOTHER TO KNIT SOCKS? I used to ponder this question.

For years I had no desire to knit socks. I had always thought of socks as a necessary evil. You wear them, you wash them, they shrivel up. After they've gone through this rotation a few times, the heel wears thin enough to justify throwing them away. Then you buy more and repeat the process. I couldn't imagine taking the time and going to the expense of knitting a pair of socks that would be worn a few times, then discarded. After all, you can buy a pack of six pairs of white tube socks at any drugstore or flea market for a couple of dollars.

But people knit socks. Some people knit nothing *but* socks. There are on-line communities devoted to the knitting of socks. There are online photo albums filled with photos of nothing but hand-knitted socks. There are scads of books of sock patterns. What did these people know that I didn't know?

Suddenly, a few years ago, a new breed of sock yarns appeared for sale. Self-patterning yarns. Yarns that made stripes and Fair Isle patterns as you knit them, as if by magic, in alluring color combinations. And most of these yarns were a blend of approximately 75% wool and 25% nylon, so they had the look and feel of pure wool, but could be machine-washed and -dried. I was intrigued. After forty-odd years of avoiding socks, I joined an e-mail group for sock devotees and started reading the messages. It was fascinating. People were discussing sock construction the way I imagine architects discuss the construction of skyscrapers. Toe-up or top-down? Short-row heel, Dutch heel, Eye of the Partridge heel? Round toe or square toe? What about grafting?

So I started surfing the Internet for sock patterns, and printed out several thousand that seemed to have possibility. Then I began my quest for the perfect yarn for my first pair of socks.

One of the companies that was touting self-patterning sock yarn was offering a colorway that captured my attention: a yarn that created tiger stripes as you knit it. How could I resist? I ordered a skein. I was a little disappointed when it arrived—a nondescript skein of faded orange/black/cream hodgepodge, wrapped with a brown-paper ball band.

But thousands of sock knitters can't be wrong, right? I whipped out the double-pointed needles, picked a pattern, knitted a tiny gauge swatch, and started in on a toe-up sock. Lo and behold, a tiger stripe started to emerge from my needles. It was fascinating! I couldn't put the needles down, so great was my excitement at seeing the tiger print develop.

A day later I had a pair of soft, lovely tiger-striped socks. Ah, but how sturdy were they? I sent them through the washer and dryer, and they emerged even softer and lovelier than before.

I went online and ordered sock yarn for ten or twelve more pairs. I ordered double-pointed needles in a variety of sizes. It was time for some serious experimentation.

I tried different toes, different heels, and different methods of finishing the cuffs. These were all toe-up socks—to this day I have yet to knit a pair of socks top-down.

My single-minded devotion to toe-up socks, by the way, stems from my hatred of certain finishing techniques. Kitchener stitch (or grafting), to be exact. It is vile. I love to knit, but hate the fiddly finishing bits.

Kitchener stitch was named after Lord Kitchener, a Boer War hero, who was apparently involved in a Red Cross plan to get women to knit socks for the troops. Legend has it that he came up with his own sock pattern with a grafted toe.

To graft a toe, you line up the stitches on two needles, thread the end of the working yarn through a tapestry needle, and weave the yarn through the "live" stitches in such a way as to make an invisible seam that simulates a continuous row of knitting.

For the life of me, I cannot remember the sequence of motions you need to go through to properly graft stitches together. This admission fills me with shame, for I am not a particularly stupid woman. I memorize things easily. I can still remember every word of my third grade Christmas pageant. But I can never, ever remember how to graft. I have to look it up every time.

If you knit a sock from the top down, you must close up the toe somehow. And, I have to admit, the best way to do that is to graft the stitches together. But if you knit a sock from the toe up, all that remains after you complete the sock is to weave in a couple of yarn ends. So toe-up socks it was.

It occurred to me early on in this experiment that sock knitting could easily be the ultimate commuter knitting.

Commuter knitting never used to be an issue for me. I live in northern Virginia and always worked in northern Virginia. I simply got in my car and drove to my office, parking in the (ahem, free) garage beneath my office building. I could easily transport to the office my regular knitting bag (containing whatever my current work in progress was) to work on during my lunch break.

Then, in the late 1990s, through a series of events that culminated in an offer I couldn't refuse, I started working for the federal government in Washington, DC. I could no longer drive my car to work, as there was simply no parking available. At any price. I started taking the subway to work, quite a jolt for a sheltered princess who had diligently avoided public transportation all her life.

It's a forty-five-minute subway trip from my home in the wilds of suburbia to my office in the heart of DC. For the first year or so, I brought paperback books to read on the commute, but reading on the train often brought on motion sickness so this was not always plausible. But I really hated the idea of wasting ninety minutes a day simply sitting on the train doing nothing. I thought: Why not knit on the train? I can knit without looking at my work— heck, I can almost knit in my sleep, so motion sickness ought not to stop me.

I started thinking about criteria for my commuter knitting. Because the subway is almost always crowded, the project had to be small enough to stuff in my purse or a small bag so I could easily carry it and access it, even when jammed in a seat with an individual who overflowed into my side of the seat with briefcases, gym bags, computers, etc. It had to be relatively mindless so I wouldn't need to refer to a pattern (see the discussion of reading causing motion sickness, above). And it had to be self-contained so I wouldn't have endless paraphernalia to fumble and drop and have roll away from me down the aisle of the train. And, heaven forbid, draw any more attention to myself than necessary.

There was, of course, something wrong with every sock pattern I had found. Each one had some little fussy detail that made it unfit for commuter knitting. First off, I eliminated all cuff-down sock patterns from consideration. Then I discarded anything with cables or lace, complicated texture stitches, or fancy heel treatments. I was not left with much.

In the online sock discussion group I was reading, many people were creating their own sock patterns and talking about the creation process. So, in the tradition of inquisitive, thinking knitters everywhere, I developed my own pattern, using the techniques and treatments that worked best for me, drawing elements from some of the existing sock patterns I had tried, as well as figuring out my own way of doing things. I got that architectural thrill from this process, creating a blueprint for a structure I was going to build. And it actually worked!

I started with a provisional cast-on for the toe, which was then created using short rows. I decided on a short-row heel as well, so I wouldn't have to pick up stitches along the heel flap. I worked out the formula and memorized it. The only prep work I had to do to embark on a sock was to crochet a chain out of waste yarn so I could start the toe. I did this at home so I wouldn't have to carry a crochet hook with me.

My commuter knitting kit now consisted of my double-pointed needles, the crocheted chain, a skein of preferably Opal sock yarn, and a business card I had measured and marked off in inches to use as a ruler. (A standard business card is exactly 3½ by 2 inches and makes a very handy portable measuring device.)

I began to knit socks on the train to and from work. I soon discovered that socks attract a lot more attention than "flat" knitting. People started striking up conversations with me about my sock in progress. This was not always a good thing, but it was always interesting. A couple of times I was told by elderly women that I was knitting the sock "wrong" because I was knitting toe-up instead of top-down. One particularly militant woman actually tried to take my sock in progress out of my hands so that she could show me how to correctly knit a sock. She quickly discovered how bad an idea that was, to the amusement of the other commuters. One day a somewhat peculiar-looking man sat down next to me.

Him: What are you knitting?

Me: A sock.

Him: A sock? Ha-ha!

Pause.

Him: It looks like you started at the toe.

Me: Yes, I did.

Him: Why?

Me: Just because. I like making them this way.

Him: What are you going to do about the heel?

Me: I've got the heel done—see? (I waved the sock at him.)

Him: Oh, so now you just have to finish it at the top.

I was impressed. This was the most thoughtful knitting conversation I'd ever had on the train. The fact that the somewhat peculiar-looking man was picking what I hoped were imaginary bugs out of his hair and eating them while discussing the finer points of sock construction did somewhat detract from the experience, though.

I bought more sock yarn. A lot more sock yarn. Every season, yarn companies come out with new colorways and patterns and I had to have them all. I discovered the concept of "limited edition" sock yarn, so I bought even more out of fear of having it disappear before I could get my hands on it.

And the needles! I learned about wooden sock needles. I bought sock needles in ebony, birch, bamboo, and rosewood. I bought short needles for little socks, longer needles for larger socks.

I now had half a dozen pairs of socks completed, but not one of these socks had yet graced a foot. They were stacked in a neat pile on my coffee table at home. I would pick them up and fondle them periodically, marveling at their color and construction. But I was loath to put sock to foot. I felt unworthy to wear works of art.

I decided that I needed to get over it. Socks should not be simply art objects, but wearable art. It was time to start inflicting my hand-knit socks on others. The first victim was Ian, my boyfriend. To his credit, he didn't even ask why I was carefully measuring the dimensions of his foot and ankle one evening, furiously calculating and making notations in a small notebook.

I decided that none of the brightly colored sock yarns I already had were appropriate for a pair of manly socks, so of course I ordered more sock yarn, this in a pale heather gray. (While I was at it, I of course ordered more brightly colored sock yarn.) I knitted a pair of plain socks with a sedate rib pattern and presented them to Ian.

He tried them on and they fit his feet perfectly. As if they had been, well, made for him. All those measurements and calculations had paid off. He wore them, good sport that he is. And to my very great surprise, he wore them a lot. He washed them a lot. He proclaimed them more comfortable than store-bought socks. And, most important, he said he wouldn't mind patterned socks in appropriate colors.

Spurred on by this sock-affirming experience, I looked for another victim upon whom I could foist my socks. The obvious (to me) choice was my friend Odie, who has "sock issues." Odie has very small feet and tiny ankles and in our frequent philosophical discussions about why things are the way they are, she had often bemoaned the fact that commercially manufactured socks simply did not fit her. They would bag around her ankles, and the seam so often present across the top of the toe actually caused her pain: it rubbed against her foot as she walked. Odie willingly offered up her foot to my tape measure.

The resulting socks were a huge success. Odie put them on and proclaimed them not only a perfect fit, but extremely comfortable and very pretty. She made a point of showing them to everyone and anyone who would look at them, telling them, "My friend Wendy custom-made these for me!"

For every gift-giving occasion that presented itself, Ian and Odie received socks. I gathered up all my coffee table socks and sent them to the Ship Project, a charity that sends knitted items to our military forces overseas.

The following Christmas, I made socks for all of my immediate family. Two days after Christmas, my mother phoned me, asking me to remind her of the sock washing instructions I had given her.

"I just now managed to get your socks away from your father and I want to wash them before he wants to wear them again. He says they are the most comfortable socks he owns."

My career as a sock knitter was flourishing. I could knit one sock per week on the train, so I was completing twenty-six pairs a year, and giving most of them away. Socks make great quickie gifts, and I discovered that they are almost universally appreciated. Sure, I've given some socks to unappreciative recipients, but it's easy to figure out who is less than enthusiastic about them, so I don't repeat the mistake. For me, socks are a labor of love, whether I am knitting them for an unknown soldier fighting overseas, for a member of my family, or for a good friend.

Some sock recipients would tell me, "I don't want to wear them because I don't want to wear them out!" I would respond, ungraciously, "If you don't wear them, I'm taking them back." No one ever gave a pair back.

I even started wearing my own hand-knit socks myself. What everyone said was true: they are very soft and comfortable to wear. I put them through the regular laundry cycle, they emerge looking lovely, and I've yet to wear out a pair.

A while back when my friend Odie was seriously ill, one of her childhood friends flew in to help her family cope with everything. When Odie was hospitalized, her friend phoned me to report on her condition. Odie had had a very bad day—invasive tests to which she had a bad reaction. When she was returned to her hospital room, the first thing she said was, "Please put Wendy's socks on my feet."

This is why I knit socks.

Wendy's Generic Toe-Up Socks

Size

Women's medium (large)

Note: You can adjust this pattern for any size, any gauge. Measure around the ball of the target foot with a tape measure. Multiply the number of inches you get by the number of stitches you get per inch when you do a gauge swatch. Then subtract 10 percent from that total. Fudge your number so it's divisible by 4. This will make a nice, snug-fitting sock. This pattern is written using 60 stitches around for the sock, with changes for 64 stitches in parentheses.

Materials

As written, this pattern calls for 100 grams of sock yarn (350 to 400 yards) to make a pair of adult socks sized for a medium foot. You'll need a tad more for larger socks, and less for smaller socks.

Gauge

8 sts = 1". I usually use five US size 0 (2mm) double-pointed needles with sock yarn, but I'm a loose knitter. Your mileage may vary, so check your gauge!

Directions

Start the toe

Using a provisional cast-on, cast on 30 (32) stitches (half the total circumference of the sock). I do my provisional cast-on using a crochet chain as follows:

Using waste yarn, crochet a chain that is several chain stitches longer than the number of knit stitches you need. Cast off the last stitch and cut the yarn. Tie a knot in this tail of yarn—you are going to "unzip" this provisional cast-on later by undoing and pulling on this end, so the knot will make the right end easier to find.

Look at your chain. One side of it will be smooth and look like a row of little Vs. The other side will have a bump in the center of each V. Using your sock yarn and two double-pointed needles, knit 1 stitch into the bump in the center of each little V on the back side of the chain until you have 30 (32) stitches.

Purl back across the stitches. You are ready to start the short rows.

Work short rows for the toe:

Row 1: Knit 29 (31) stitches. Move the working yarn as if to purl. Slip the last, unworked stitch from the left needle to the right needle. Turn your work.

Row 2: Slip the first, unworked stitch from the left needle to the right needle. Purl the next stitch (you will have wrapped that first stitch around its base with the working yarn) and purl across to the last stitch. Move the working yarn as if to knit and slip last stitch. Turn.

Row 3: Slip the first stitch and knit across to the last stitch before the unworked stitch. Wrap and turn.

Row 4: Slip the first stitch and purl across to the stitch before the unworked stitch. Wrap and turn.

Repeat rows 3 and 4 until 8 (9) of the toe stitches are wrapped and on the left side, 14 (14) stitches are "live" in the middle, and 8 (9) are wrapped and on the right. At this stage, you should be ready to work a right side row. Your toe is half done.

Note: How many stitches you leave unworked in the middle depends on how wide you want your sock toe to be. If you want it a bit wider, do a couple fewer short rows. If you want it a bit narrower, do a couple more short rows.

Now you'll work the second half of the toe:

Continue the toe:

Row 1: Knit across the 14 (14) live stitches across to the first unworked, wrapped stitch. To work this stitch, pick up the wrap and knit it together with the stitch. Wrap the next stitch (so that it now has two wraps) and turn.

Row 2: Slip the first (double-wrapped) stitch and purl across to the first unworked, wrapped stitch. Pick up the wrap and purl it together with the stitch. Wrap the next stitch and turn.

On subsequent rows you will pick up both wraps and knit or purl them together with the stitch.

Continue until you have worked all the stitches and you once again have 30 (32) "live" stitches.

When all 30 (32) stitches are once again "live," divide those stitches over two needles. Unzip your provisional cast-on and divide those 30 (32) stitches over two more needles. On your first round, you may want to pick up an extra stitch or two between the "live" stitches and the stitches you've picked up from the cast-on, to close up any holes that might be there. On the next round remember to decrease back down to 15 (16) stitches per needle.

Note: Insert the tip of your needle into the stitch you knit up from the provisional cast-on before you unzip the chain—this will make it much easier to pick up the loops of the stitches. I usually insert my needle through four or five loops at a time, unzip the chain from them, do the next four or five loops, unzip, until I've picked them all up. When you un-zip your provisional cast-on, you will have one less stitch than the total you picked up and knit. You can create that extra stitch at the end by pick-ing up the loop between the last stitch created with the provisional cast-on and the first live stitch.

You now have a total of 60 (64) stitches.

Form the instep:

Work straight until the foot is about 2" shorter than the desired finished length. Place the 30 (32) instep stitches on one needle and put the 30 (32) heel stitches on another needle. Work a short-row heel on the 30 (32) heel stitches the same way you did the short-row toe, as follows.

Work short rows for the heel:

Row 1: Knit 29 (31) stitches. Move the working yarn as if to purl. Slip the last, unworked stitch from the left needle to the right needle. Turn your work.

Row 2: Slip the first, unworked stitch from the left needle to the right needle. Purl the next stitch (you will have wrapped that first stitch around its base with the working yarn) and purl across to the last stitch. Move the working yarn as if to knit and slip last stitch. Turn.

Row 3: Slip the first stitch and knit across to the last stitch before the un-worked stitch. Wrap and turn.

Row 4: Slip the first stitch and purl across to the stitch before the un-worked stitch. Wrap and turn.

Repeat rows 3 and 4 until 8 (9) of the heel stitches are wrapped and on the left side, 14 (14) stitches are "live" in the middle, and 8 (9) are wrapped and on the right. At this stage, you should be ready to work a right side row. Your heel is half done.

Note: How many stitches you leave unworked in the middle depends on how wide you want your sock heel to be. If you want it a bit wider, do a couple fewer short rows. If you want it a bit narrower, do a couple more short rows.

Now you'll work the second half of the heel:

Continue the heel:

Row 1: Knit across the 14 (14) live stitches across to the first unworked, wrapped stitch. To work this stitch, pick up the wrap and knit it together with the stitch. Wrap the next stitch (so that it now has two wraps) and turn.

Row 2: Slip the first (double-wrapped) stitch and purl across to the first unworked, wrapped stitch. Pick up the wrap and purl it together with the stitch. Wrap the next stitch and turn.

On subsequent rows you will pick up both wraps and knit or purl them together with the stitch.

Continue until you have worked all the stitches and you once again have 30 (32) "live" stitches.

When you have all stitches live again, divide the stitches as you did for the toe. Once again, on your first round, you may want to pick up an extra stitch or two between the "live" stitches and the stitches you left on a needle for the instep, to close up any holes that might be there. On the next round remember to decrease back down to 15 (16) stitches per needle.

Form the ankle and cuff:

Work until the leg is the desired length to the ribbing, then work in ribbing to the desired finished length.

Cast off loosely.

Note: Individuals with wide feet and/or heavier legs might find it difficult to get socks on and off. I sometimes increase stitches when I start the ribbing for the cuff. If I start out with 15 stitches per needle, I'll increase to 16 stitches per needle, and do a k4 p4 rib. If I start out with 16 stitches per needle, I'll increase to 18 stitches per needle, and do a k3 p3 rib. As you can see, it's not an exact science—you can fudge wherever you feel the need to, to suit the socks' recipient.

Chapter 7 • There's No Crying in Knitting!

ONE OF THE MOST FRUSTRATING SIDE EFFECTS of knitting is making mistakes. There's nothing more discouraging and disheartening for a beginner knitter (or any knitter, for that matter) than laboring long hours over a project only to discover a dropped or misworked stitch several rows down. Or to finish a sweater for yourself and discover that it's either too small or so large that you and several of your friends, as a group, could easily wear it.

Mistakes? I've made them all. And through all those mistakes I've learned how to "read" my knitting so I can recognize mistakes as they happen. I've figured out how to fix mistakes without having to rip back. I've also learned that sometimes it's okay to ignore mistakes, live with them, and call them a "design element." This is what I like to call the "I Meant to Do That" school of knitting.

Let's start with a classic mistake, which hardly qualifies as a mistake. It is more of a universal state of being: buying too little yarn for the project, or misplacing a skein or two. The bottom line is that you run short of yarn. We've probably all done this. I think that this might just be a rite of passage for knitters, a constant of the universe. It is the hazing that one must go through to be deemed worthy to bear the title of "knitter." When you have worked through and survived your first yarn shortage crisis, you are on your way. Nay, you have arrived!

I learned about that faux pas early on, when I was a child. My mom was making a Scandinavian-style ski sweater. You know the type, snowflake motifs on a plain background. White snowflakes on a red background, in this case. Mom had knitted the entire sweater and, on the sleeve cap for the last sleeve, ran out of the red yarn. I don't remember the exact circumstances of this knit. Perhaps the yarn was some that she had had in her stash for a while, or the color was no longer available. Whatever it was, she resigned herself to having to make do with a completely different yarn in as close a shade of red as she could find. She completed the last sleeve in a slightly different red. It wasn't terribly noticeable, unless you looked for it.

I used to borrow the sweater when I was in high school and, in moments of adolescent ennui, gaze at that "off" red until my eyes glazed over. It's a wonder I managed to graduate high school.

This little patch of red yarn was a great early lesson. It's okay if you make a mistake. Heck, if my mom could make a mistake, I could too.*

Oh, the angst of running out of yarn! It used to happen to me a lot. It still does occasionally. And I am not the only one. On knitting e-mail lists and online knitting message boards, you see the frantic pleas almost every day: "I need one skein of Debbie Bliss Cotton Cashmere yarn, in color number 15007, pink, dye lot number 11." And that's the divine thing about the Internet: there's often someone out there, reading that message, who has exactly what you are looking for and is willing to sell or trade.

Running short of yarn most often happens to me when I substitute yarns, which I do often. Sometimes the recommended yarn is discontinued or un-

---

*Sorry, Mom, but I had to "out" you and your mistake there. It was my first experience with yarn shortage and it's for the good of the knitters.

available, or it's expensive and I am too cheap to plunk down the bucks for it. Perhaps I don't like any of the colors available for the recommended yarn.

But when you substitute yarns you are just asking for trouble.

Case in point: I bought some lovely wool yarn from an online auction. It had been long discontinued, so long that I could find no information about the yarn in an online search. And the information on the yarn's ball band was sketchy at best. There was no yardage information listed. Still, it was pretty, a soft heathered beige, and I wanted to use it for a particular pattern: a crewneck Aran pullover.

I started knitting, and the agony began. Am I going to have enough? Am I going to have enough? This phrase played on an endless loop in my brain. I agonized about the yarn when I was awake and I dreamed about the yarn when I slept. In my dream, I was knitting frantically and my yarn was diminishing, yet the knitted piece did not grow.

I finished the back of the sweater. I had ten skeins of yarn and the back took about three and a half of them. Hmmm, I thought. The front will take slightly less than the back. That's under seven skeins. Will three skeins be enough for the sleeves?

For the record, three skeins were not enough for the sleeves. To this day, this sweater remains in its unfinished state. The last sleeve is only half done, its live stitches on a holder, never to be completed. The yarn appears to be available nowhere on earth. And to be honest, at this point I've forgotten what yarn it was.

Another sad story: I was knitting an Aran pullover from a wool yarn I had bought from a mail-order source, Bovidae Farm, a small independent retailer. On the last sleeve, I ran out of yarn. I ordered some more, but was told that they no longer had the dye lot I had bought. This yarn was from another dye lot, they warned me—was that okay? Sure, how different could it be? I thought.

The answer was: very different. Dramatically different. But I had no choice, so I finished the sweater with the different dye lot yarn. Then I gave the sweater away (to someone who didn't notice the different dye lot, or was at least too polite to mention it) because the sight of the two-toned sleeve made me sad.

After a couple of close calls and a couple more outright disasters, I learned to always buy a couple of extra balls when subbing yarn. I can live with that. I do so enjoy substituting yarns. It makes the knitting of a sweater that much more exciting, seeing how the yarn I've chosen will work with the design. I call this "life on the edge." Others may well call it "sad."

If I think I'm cutting it close with the amount of yarn I have, I knit the back, and then a sleeve. That accounts for approximately half the yarn needed for the entire sweater, unless you are knitting a design with a really big collar. If you've used over half of your yarn, you are going to need more. It's as simple as that.

The generosity of yarn allowed for a pattern required varies widely, depending on the designer. I went through a spell of knitting sweaters from patterns published by Dale of Norway, buying the exact yarn in the exact amounts recommended in the pattern. Without fail, I always ran short of yarn and had to buy more. I finally wrote to the company about the constant yarn shortages in their patterns, and they wrote back, telling me that each design was knitted only in one size, and the yarn requirements for all other sizes extrapolated from that. This is very good information to have, and ever since then, I've bought extra yarn when knitting one of this company's patterns. And every single time, I've needed the extra yarn. So I learned that pattern information is by no means infallible.

Nowadays, whenever I knit a design from an unknown designer, that is, one whose designs I've never knitted, I almost always buy an extra skein or two. In most cases I don't need the extra yarn, but once in a while I do. And if I fail to buy extra, of course, I will always run short. This is one of those constants in the universe, like the phenomenon of dropping a piece of toast and having it always land butter and jam-side down.

If you are substituting a different yarn for a pattern, look at the particulars of the yarn the pattern calls for: the gauge, the size (weight) of each skein, and the yardage for each skein. For example, your pattern calls for 16 skeins of Debbie Bliss Cashmerino Aran, a worsted-weight yarn with 100 yards per 50-gram skein. Multiply the number of yards (or meters) per skein by the number of skeins called for and there you have the total yardage needed for the design (in this case, 16 times 100, for a total of 1,600 yards). Divide that number by the number of yards per skein of the yarn you are actually planning on using to make the design, and then add one more skein, just for insurance. For example, you might want to substitute Dale of Norway Falk, which has 88 yards per 50-gram skein. Divide 1,600 by 88 and you get 18.18 skeins. I'd buy 19 skeins to be on the safe side. When I do this, I never run short. At least I haven't yet.

But running out of yarn is just the beginning in the Great Pantheon of Knitting Errors.

Another common mistake is making a sweater that does not fit. I cannot tell you how many times I've labored over a knitting project for weeks and weeks, finally completed it, tried it on, and . . . it looks terrible. Because it's too big, too small, or just wrong for me.

Fit is directly affected by your gauge (the number of stitches per inch), and bad gauge is often the cause of badly sized sweaters.

If you have a pattern for a sweater that is supposed to be knitted at

5 stitches to the inch, and you knit it at 4 stitches to the inch, you're in for a very big surprise indeed when you try it on. If you knit a sweater that has 200 stitches in circumference, at 5 stitches to the inch you'll have a completed sweater with a chest measurement of 40 inches. At 4 stitches to the inch, your 200-stitch-around sweater measures 50 inches around! Quite a difference there! Heck, if you knit it at a gauge of 4.75 stitches to the inch, your sweater will end up just over 42 inches around. A quarter of a stitch per inch makes a difference, as you can plainly see.

This happened to me a lot in my younger days, when I had a blatant disregard for gauge. I was very cavalier. If I was close, I figured I was okay—until I realized that close doesn't cut it.

There was one occasion, when I was very young, when I arrogantly knitted a sweater with the aforementioned blatant disregard for gauge. I believe I was using a chunky-weight yarn with a pattern that specified worsted weight. The resulting sweater looked like a pup tent. The fact that it was a bilious pea green had nothing to do with the gauge problems but, as I recall, did nothing to enhance the sweater's appearance.

What I should have done when I finished this monstrosity was rip it out and use the yarn for something more suitable for its gauge. That's what I should have done. But no. I decided to take the sweater in along the side seams and leave the several extra inches bunched up on the inside, sewing it up with my less-than-stellar back-stitching. I'm sure you can imagine what this poor sweater looked like when it was done. It was even more uncomfortable to actually wear, so I relegated it to the rag pile and it became a cat blanket. I was surprised the cat deigned to sleep on it. Generally he had better taste.

The other important thing to remember is that you can knit a sweater, exactly to gauge, and it still looks lousy on you. Go on, ask me how I know this.

Of course, sometimes the answer is obvious. If you are five-foot-nothing and slender, an oversized sweater with drop shoulders will most likely not be a flattering look for you.

If you've got a good idea of the type of stuff that looks good on you, and keep that in mind when choosing a pattern to knit, you'll likely end up with sweaters you like. I know what styles are most flattering to me and try to stick to knitting designs in these styles. When I deviate from this and knit something that looks cute but simply is not my style, I am always, without fail, disappointed.

Take a good look at the sweater pictured on the pattern. If the model is coyly holding a bunch of flowers or another prop in a strategic position, it is quite possible that the photo stylist is covering up an atrocity in the sweater design. I am always suspicious of overly artsy layouts and odd poses in pattern pictures, as I always assume they are trying to distract my eye from some design deficiency. Of course, I do have an overly suspicious nature, but when I'm right, I'm usually right.

And another rule of thumb I go by: if it doesn't look good on a slinky, eighty-pound model, it is not going to look good on me. I love patterns that picture the sweater on a "real" person. Then, I figure, there is a ghost of a chance that the design will look becoming on me as well.

The question of ease is important as well. I like comfortable clothes, so therefore, I don't like sweaters that fit tightly. If you are unsure of how much ease to allow, measure a sweater that you think fits you well and that you are comfortable wearing, and use those measurements when choosing what size to knit. I find for a standard-fitting sweater, I like about four inches of ease. This always surprises me, as I think it sounds like more than it ought to be. But this is my "comfort" number, and I am always happy with the results when I stick to it.

A lot of intrepid, disciplined souls (read: masochistic) rip out sweaters that don't fit and start over. I am in awe of people who will knit something, find it not to their liking, rip it out, alter the pattern, and knit the blame thing again. Not me. I am far too impatient. I just give the sweater to someone it will fit. Or, if it is really ugly, someone against whom I am holding a grudge. "Here, I made this sweater just for *you*!" (Please don't tell.)

I abhor ripping out work. It just seems to me to be so counterproductive. I'll do almost anything to avoid it. Also, once I've completed a sweater, there is no way I'm going to reknit it. The shiny newness, the magic, the enchantment are gone and no amount of rationalization on my part about how much I would love the sweater if I just reknit it with a few modifications will change that.

There are a few patterns that I have knitted multiple times, true, but never one right after another. It's a good thing I don't have identical twins that I want to dress in matching outfits because those poor kids would never get hand-knitted sweaters made by me.

I will, however, rip out errors. Within reason. So, you ask, what is reasonable?

If I discover an error in a texture or cable pattern, I will rip down just the stitches that are involved in the incident, fix the error, and then work the ripped stitches back up to the current position. Early on I discovered that you can drop a stitch down several rows until you get to the offending stitch. Then you can use a crochet hook to pick up the stitch properly and work it back up, row by row, to the current row. If it's thick enough yarn at a loose gauge, I can do this without a crochet hook, just using my fingers.

I once made a knitted dress based on a traditional English gansey pattern. It had a zigzag texture pattern worked down the length of it in seed stitch. (I realize that this description sounds alarmingly ugly, but the design was really quite subtle and attractive.) After completing most of the body of the dress, I discovered a misworked stitch—a purl that should have been a knit—in the zigzag at least eighteen inches down.

In cases like this, I think long and hard about whether to fix the error.

Sometimes, if it's not too noticeable, I'll just pretend I didn't see the error and forge on. However, I was knitting this project from a light-colored wool, and the error really stood out, glowing like a beacon in the dark of night. It's funny that I didn't notice it until I was eighteen inches beyond the point where I made the mistake, but once I did notice it, I couldn't look away. I ripped two stitches down eighteen inches to the error and fixed it, then worked those two stitches all the way back up, using the trusty size F crochet hook I keep in my knitting bag. This operation took the better part of an evening.

I'm not saying I would recommend this as a viable solution. Sometimes ripping back is your only solution. But I was a desperate woman, a woman on the edge. And I was lucky in this case. The yarn was resilient and forgiving, and when I finished abusing it with the crochet hook, you really couldn't tell how much it had been manhandled. Because it was such a blatant error and it would have driven me nuts had I left it in, I was prepared to rip back, if need be, so what did I have to lose? Happily, my crochet hook trick worked, so the fix was achieved in an evening. It would have taken me several days to rip out and rework.

I once knitted an Aran sweater that had seventy billion trillion tiny two-stitch cable crosses. Done in twisted stitches, no less. After completing the work, I did notice a couple of those cables were crossed the wrong way. Did I fix them? Not on your life. And I defy anyone to glance at the sweater, see those incorrectly crossed cables immediately, and gasp in horror. But of course, if anyone ever does, the shame will eat at me and I will never wear the sweater again.

When I make a mistake of just a stitch or two in knitting with more than one color, it's much, much easier to cover up. I simply duplicate-stitch over the offending stitches and no one is the wiser. Duplicate stitching is a wonderful tool to have in your repertoire. You simply thread a tapestry needle with yarn in the proper color and embroider over the stitch that is in the wrong color. Anchor the ends of the new yarn securely on the wrong side of the work and you are done.

I have, however, made huge, honking mistakes in color work. Here is the worst one.

I was knitting a Fair Isle cardigan at a gauge of 8 stitches to the inch, and after several weeks of furious knitting, was coming down the home stretch: the last sleeve. I had knitted the front bands, I had knitted the collar. At this point, I was heartily sick and tired of knitting this monster and was thinking ahead to my next project (which, because I am a glutton for punishment, was another colorwork design). Only after I completed the last cuff and cast off did I notice that I'd used the wrong background color for the last inch above the cuff.

I thought long and hard about this. After having just completed the sweater, and feeling the glow of triumph and victory that comes with completing such a sweater, I really, really did not want to rip out and reknit the last four inches. Apart from the fact that ripping out Fair Isle work in Shetland wool is quite tedious, I think it is also the kind of activity that sucks out your soul. Shetland wool is quite hairy and sticks to itself with a mad passion. In my experience, it does not take kindly to being ripped out, and the cuff was worked in corrugated two-color ribbing, which is in my top two most hated things to do in knitting.

(What is my number one most hated thing to do in knitting? Two-color garter stitch. It's even more tedious and mind-numbing than corrugated ribbing, in my opinion.)

I tried to look at the sweater objectively. Would anyone really notice the inch of illicit background color? I decided that no one would.

And to this day, no one has. Sometimes I even forget about it myself. For a minute or two.

Speaking of the dreaded corrugated ribbing, I once cast on for a Fair Isle cardigan, joined the stitches, as it was being knitted in the round, and started working the painstakingly boring corrugated ribbing. (Have I mentioned that I have no affinity for corrugated ribbing? Its only saving grace, as far as I'm concerned, is that it looks so darned nice. And that is the only reason why I will consent to knit it.)

Anyhow, I had worked perhaps 5 rounds of the ribbing when it became apparent that I had twisted my stitches when I joined them at the beginning. This resulted in a twist in the knitting that made the whole thing look like a Möbius strip. A Möbius strip gone wrong.

Five rounds doesn't sound like a big deal, but what we are talking about is in excess of 300 stitches per round here, and slow-going ones at that. What do you do in a situation like this?

The only thing that saved me from having to rip the whole mess out was that I was knitting a cardigan. A cardigan knitted in the round employs a steek, an area of several stitches, down the front of the entire body, where you may cut the piece open later and pick up stitches and knit the front bands.

I cut the sweater (less than an inch at this point) open right down the center of the steek stitches, untwisted my work, and then simply rejoined and continued knitting. So I had a tiny bit of precut steek when I was done, and no one was the wiser.

And since that happened, I have been compulsive about checking my cast-on stitches to ensure that they are not twisted. An ounce of prevention, blah, blah, blah.

I am guilty of having made bonehead, embarrassing mistakes as well. My most memorable of those happened on a pair of mittens.

My mom used to make beautiful two-color mittens for us when we were kids, patterned with Scandinavian snowflake motifs and with the recipient's name knitted on the back of the mitten just above the cuff.

When I was in college I decided to knit a pair as a holiday gift for my best friend, Ann. I laboriously charted her (thankfully short) name so I could personalize them as my mom had always done. (If her name had been Hermione or Alexandra or something like that, her mittens would have remained anonymous.)

I finished the first mitten and was delighted with the results. I set it aside and eagerly cast on the second mitten. It wasn't long before I had it done. Mittens are fast and fun to knit, and this pair was made from worsted-weight yarn, which works up quickly.

It was only after completing the second mitten that I realized I had made two right-hand mittens.

There are some patterns for mittens that have you make the thumb sticking out the side of the mitten, so you make two identical. Not so with these. The thumb on these mittens is offset on the palm, so the mittens are not interchangeable. Besides, there was a different pattern on the palm of the mitten than was on the back. It was a fine mess.

I remember exactly what I did when I discovered my mistake. I threw a tantrum. I jumped up and down and screamed and hollered, and then I actually took a pair of scissors to the poor mittens and butchered them. Then I went out and bought my friend a gift. I do not remember what I bought her, but it was not a pair of mittens.

Not once did it cross my mind that it would only take a couple of days, perhaps only ten hours' work, to reknit the second mitten. This is testament to my hatred of having to do anything over.

I have, however, grown up a little since the mitten incident. Now, when I make horrific, bonehead errors, I suck it up, rip out, and reknit. That, or I toss the whole project to one side and pretend it never existed. (Denial over de-knitting.) Once I even ripped out an entire sweater after deeming it not flattering for me, and used the yarn to knit a different design. This is a rarity for me, as I am supremely lazy. It is a testament to how much I liked that particular yarn.

There are other mistakes you can make when the knitting is done. Washing the sweater springs immediately to mind.

How many of you have had a "hand wash only" sweater thrown in the washing machine and have it come out ruined beyond repair? This is through no fault of your own, of course. You can always blame the husband, the housemate, or the kids for this transgression.

I remember an incident of this sort from my childhood. My mother was taking the clothes out of the washing machine and discovered that a wool sweater had gotten mixed in with the laundry. When she pulled it out of the washing machine after the hot cycle, the only one it would have fit was the family cat.

In a case like this, I'm sorry to say, you are probably screwed. The sweater is most likely "felted" beyond repair. The only thing you can do with it (should your family cat not wish to wear it) is perhaps cut it up to make a pillow, a purse, coasters, or potholders. And let it be a reminder to you to gently hand wash your wool sweaters in lukewarm water, using a mild soap.

There are many mistakes that await us all—but my favorite balm for recovering a soul-sucking blow delivered by a difficult knit is to knit something fast and fun. The Laura Pullover is such a knit. It will soothe your injured psyche if you choose to knit it with the recommended yarn, I guarantee. After all, you deserve something fabulous, and alpaca silk yarn fits the bill.

If it doesn't fit you when you complete it, don't bother to rip it out and knit it over, unless you really want to. Please give it to someone as a gift, with my blessing.

Laura Pullover

Finished Measurements

36 (40, 44)" chest
24" length

Materials

10 (11, 13) skeins Debbie Bliss Alpaca Silk (80% alpaca, 20% silk, 72yd/50g skein)
US size 8 (5mm) needles: 1 24" circular or 1 pair straight and 1 16" circular

Gauge

18 sts and 24 rows = 4", measured over stockinette stitch using size 8 needles

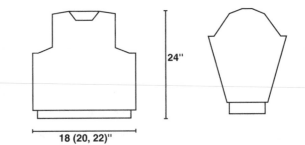

Directions

Back

Using 24" circular or straight needles, cast on 80 (90, 100) stitches. Work twisted rib as follows:

Row 1: (K1tbl, p1) to end.

Row 2: (P1tbl, k1) to end.

Work a total of 16 rows in twisted rib.

Next row (RS): Knit across, increasing 10 stitches evenly across—90 (100, 110) stitches.

Work straight in stockinette stitch until piece measures 14" from the cast-on edge.

Shape armholes:

Bind off 9 stitches at the beginning of the next 2 rows.

Decrease 1 stitch at each end on the next row, and every alternate row, a total of 8 times—56 (66, 76) stitches.

Work straight until piece measures 23½", from the cast-on edge.

Shape shoulders:

Bind off 4 (5, 6) stitches at the beginning of the next 2 rows.

Bind off 4 (6, 8) stitches at the beginning of the next 4 rows.

Bind off 32 back neck stitches.

Front

Work as for back, including all shaping, and *at the same time* when piece measures 22":

Begin neck shaping:

On next row, work 15 (20, 25) stitches, attach another ball of yarn, bind off the center 26 stitches and work across row.

Working both sides at once, decrease 1 stitch at each neck edge every other row 3 times.

Continue straight until piece measures 23½" from the cast-on edge.

Shape shoulders:

Work shoulder shaping to correspond with back.

Sleeves

Cast on 40 stitches. Work twisted rib as follows:

Row 1: (K1tbl, p1) to end.

Row 2: (P1tbl, k1) to end.

Work a total of 16 rows in twisted rib.

Next row (RS): K8 (inc1, k8) 4 times—44 stitches.

Work in stockinette stitch and increase 1 stitch at each end every 4th row until there are a total of 82 stitches. Work even until piece measures 17" from beginning.

Shape sleeve cap:

Bind off 9 stitches at the beginning of the next 2 rows.

Decrease 1 stitch at each end on every row for the next 4 rows.

Decrease 1 stitch at each end on every other row 14 times.

Bind off remaining 28 stitches.

Join front and back together at the shoulders.

Neckband

Starting at the right shoulder neck edge with the 16" circular needle, pick up 3 stitches down the right back neck, 32 stitches across the back neck, 3 stitches up the left back neck, 8 stitches down the left front neck, 26 stitches across the front neck, and 8 stitches up the right front neck—80 stitches.

Work twisted rib as follows:

Row 1: (K1tbl, p1) to end.

Row 2: (P1tbl, k1) to end.

Work a total of 8 rows in twisted rib and bind off in twisted rib.

Finishing

Weave in all loose ends and steam-press your work lightly from the wrong side. Set in the sleeves and sew up the side seams.

Chapter 8 • Needles and Numbers

A LOT OF ONE'S GOOD KNITTING KARMA, I believe, depends on having the right stuff. Because I am who I am, I obsess about everything. I love tools and I amass them happily. This is as true of knitting tools as anything else.

The most basic of knitting tools? That would be knitting needles, of course.

There are a million needles out there in the naked city and most (if not all) of them are perfect for something. Needles come in many different flavors: straights, circulars, double-points, and the somewhat odd flex needles. They are made from many different materials: metal, plastic, wood, casein, to name a few. You will have far more success in your knitting using needles that are appropriate for your yarn and project.

When I first started knitting, I borrowed and used my mother's straight metal needles. These were vintage 1950s or earlier. In the 1970s my mother bought me my own set of straight metal needles, which I used for years. At this point I'd never even seen a circular needle, much less knitted with one.

In the mid-1980s on a trip to London, I bought a set of Aero brand straight needles in a lovely yarn shop on Oxford Street, now sadly closed. They came in a red vinyl zippered case, and ranged in size from about 2mm to 5mm. When I acquired these, I used them exclusively. A year or so later I bought a set of straight bamboo needles that came in a fabric roll, also when I was in London. I was there on vacation and had neglected to bring a knitting project with me. What was I thinking? I've not made that mistake again. I bought yarn and these needles to tide me over.

I used the bamboo needles briefly when I returned home, but discovered that my cat liked to chew on the ends, so I quickly gave them to a knitting friend who was catless.

At some point soon after this I switched to using circular needles for almost all knitting. I bought Susan Bates "Quicksilver" needles and used them for years. These days I'm a die-hard circular needle user. Why knit flat using circulars? While you work, the knitted piece is not hanging off the ends of your two straight needles; rather, the weight of it is distributed along the cable of the circular needle. And the less weight I'm holding up with my two hands, the better. Also, circulars are much more conducive to knitting in confined spaces, like on the train. There are no needle ends to poke the person next to you. (Though that might not necessarily be a bad thing, depending on the person sitting next to you.)

When I started subscribing to knitting magazines and paying attention to the larger world of needles, I heard about Addi Turbo needles, which were supposed to be very "fast" needles, smooth so that the stitches slide along the needle with no resistance. I'm all for speeding things up, so I started acquiring Addi Turbos in every size and needle length. What's more is they worked—for certain projects. I do love my Addi Turbos and I use them for a lot of my knitting. But for color work, nothing beats a wooden needle.

A wooden needle has a slight amount of "grab" to it, which makes it great for Fair Isle and Norwegian designs. One of the hardest things to do in color work, I find, is to maintain an even tension throughout while changing colors, and the "grab" of the wooden needle helps you to spread out your stitches evenly and keep the tension consistent.

The most common wooden circular needles are made from bamboo, and you can find them manufactured by several different companies. Which ones work best for you is often a matter of personal preference. Some have pointier tips, some more rounded. The joins (where the wooden needle is attached to the plastic cord) are different on different brands of needles. I prefer Addi Naturas or Clover bamboos, both of which have good joins.

There are "high-end" wooden needles as well, those made from rosewood and ebony. I'd never knitted with an ebony needle until a few years ago, when an online friend mentioned that she loved them for Fair Isle. That was enough for me: I found them online and ordered a 24" US size 3 (3.25mm) Holtz & Stein ebony circular needle.

Wow. For me, this is the Maserati of knitting needles. The ebony has a feel of pure luxury that, in my opinion, no other needle can match. I've tried the rosewood needles as well and they are lovely, but my heart belongs to the ebony needles.

So of course I ordered more. I ordered as many as I could find, in as many sizes as I could find. This, sadly, was not too many. The Holtz & Stein needles were somewhat hard to find, and lately I have been unsuccessful in finding them at all in the United States. The US size 3 (3.25mm) is virtually extinct.

You can imagine my distress then when one day I picked up my precious 32" size 3 ebony needle one day and discovered that it was chipped. It was not a small chip. A huge chunk was missing from the tip. While I could probably have filed down the end, I doubt I could have restored the needle to its former glory. As the size 3 is the size I use most often, I mourned.

A month or so later I got a package in the mail from an online friend in Germany. Inside were not one but two 32" size 3 circular ebony needles. I shrieked with delight when I opened the package, frightening those within earshot. It's hard to explain to someone who has never used ebony knitting needles the feeling of security that you experience knowing you have a needle plus a spare in your most often used size.

So I guard my precious ebonies jealously now, and treat them with the utmost care and respect. I hope against hope that someone will make them readily available in the United States again soon.

As I've expressed, I use circulars a lot, but not for everything. For socks I much prefer double-pointed needles (dpns). When I first started knitting socks, I used metal dpns, but I had a lot of problems with the needles sliding out of my work because they were so smooth and slippery. This was very annoying, particularly when I knit on the train. It's hard to maintain that sangfroid you have worked so hard to achieve when you've got steel needles clanging to the floor of the train car. I bought some 8" bamboo dpns and used them for a while. But the 8" length was just a bit too long—I always had the fear (or temptation) of stabbing my neighbor when I used them. I did some research and discovered Pony Pearl dpns. Made from a plastic material, they came in a 15cm length, which is about 5½". I used these happily for my socks. I used them happily, that is, until I discovered a shorter needle: the Brittany Birch 5" dpns.

These little guys are perfect for me for knitting socks and gloves. The only caution I will offer is that they are fragile in the smaller sizes, as are all wooden needles. I knit most of my socks on US size 0 (2mm) needles, so I quickly got used to treating my tiny needles with care. The smaller-size wooden needles can warp with use and age as well, but that doesn't bother me.

What does bother me is the strange obsession that my cat Lucy has with small wooden needles.

I was knitting a glove using my size 0 Brittany Birch dpns, and took it to bed with me. While I realize this may sound odd and perhaps a bit pathetic, I was planning on watching television for a while before falling asleep and I was almost finished with the glove. I figured I could complete it that night.

Well, finish it I did, and I left the glove on my nightstand, along with the remainder of the ball of yarn, in which I carefully stuck the 5" dpns, and went to sleep. When I woke up in the morning, the glove was still there, but the ball of yarn, along with the dpns, was missing.

I found the ball of yarn in the living room with the dpns still stuck in it. But sadly, on closer inspection I discovered that one of the dpns was splintered and broken. Lucy feigned innocence, but I knew she was responsible. Fortunately, I had another identical set of these birch dpns, but the memory of the broken needle remains a bitter one.

The moral of that story is to never, ever leave your needles where your pet (or your child, I suppose) can get at them.

This brings me to an important question: How do you store your needles?

Some of my needles came in sets, and are housed in their own cases. My Pony Pearl dpns live in a fabric needle roll that a friend made and gave to me. But I have many more needles than these.

I started out keeping all the circulars in a drawer in a cabinet in my stash room, but found that inconvenient, because every time I wanted a different needle, I had to get up, go in the stash room, and rummage around to get it. So I started keeping all my circulars (in their individual plastic bags) in a basket that sat by my "knitting spot" on the couch. The dpns had their own separate basket.

But I amassed more needles. (You know how that goes. Your 24" size 7 circular is in use, and you want to start another project. So you buy another one. And then you need a 16" circular for the sleeves and the neckband; and on and on.) Before I knew it, I had many more needles, so I bought some accordion files and used a pocket for each needle size. But of course, the accordion file got filled up quickly.

My current solution works very well for me. I went to an office supply store and bought a "tower" of drawers—a plastic cabinet on wheels that has ten drawers. Drawers 1 through 8 hold needle sizes (both circulars and dpns) 0 through 7. Drawer 9 holds sizes 8 and 9, and the bottom drawer has all my larger-size needles. This has been working perfectly for me for well over a year. I have more size 3 needles (from knitting lots of Fair Isle) than any other size, and they still fit nicely in one drawer, with room for more.

But there's much more to knitting tools than needles. I have a love-hate relationship with row counters.

Like many, I depend on row counters to keep track of my knitting. And like many, I carry my knitting most everywhere I go. Therefore, I need to carry my row counter everywhere I go. The easiest way to do this is to have a row counter that is attached to my knitting. Sounds easy enough, right?

I have a number of those little counters that fit on the needle. You know the kind: they are barrel-shaped and display two digits. You twist the ends to advance the numbers. They are made for straight needles, but you can slide one onto one end of your circular needle and let it hang on the cable, assuming you are using a circular to knit back and forth.

However, I have some issues with these counters. Some of the barrel counters in my possession have a turning mechanism that is too loose, so the numbers whirl around with the slightest touch, while others have turning mechanisms that are too tight, so it takes a lot of effort to advance the number. Such a bother.

At this moment, I have exactly one old Aero barrel counter that is just right. The turning mechanism has the perfect amount of tension so you can advance it fairly easily, but it does not advance on its own. I treat it like the precious object that it is. If I lose it, or if it loses its perfect tension, well, I don't know what I'll do.

Truthfully, I do know what I'll do. I'll resort to a "kacha-kacha" counter. One of those rectangular plastic counters that you click to advance the numbers. I do possess one of these, but use it very infrequently, because it can't be attached to my knitting, and therefore I am likely to forget it.

I understand that there is an electronic row counter now being made, though I've not seen one in person. Strangely this does not appeal to me. I say strangely, because I am a sucker for electronic gadgets. I think if this counter had audio, a voice (preferably James Earl Jones's voice) that intoned the row numbers as you clicked them off ("This . . . is Row Number One"), it would have far more appeal for me.

Every knitter also needs stitch holders. Often you need someplace to put live stitches that you are going to use later. Granted, you can thread them onto a length of yarn and use that as a holder, but transferring stitches to a stitch holder is faster. You can, of course, also use a spare circular needle to hold stitches. But then you've got a circular needle with the ends hanging out, flopping about like a fish out of water. As you have probably figured out by now, I prefer a stitch holder.

All my stitch holders are the same type, and I believe they are obsolete. I prefer to think of them as valuable heirlooms, but at any rate, I haven't seen any like them in years. They were made by Aero, and consist of a metal needle, on which you slide the stitches, with a spring attached at one end. There's a cap at the other end of the spring, so you can cap the end of the needle and keep the stitches on the holder. The spring keeps the cap on. I have these holders in three sizes.

Before I got these, I used the type that resembles a large safety pin. I never liked this sort of stitch holder, as it was possible for stitches to escape off the business end.

I've recently noticed a "new breed" of stitch holders—double-ended ones, so you can remove the cap and access your stitches from either end of the holder. What a brilliant concept! I may have to invest in some of these. Because my stitch holders have the removable cap at one end only, they are "one-way" stitch holders. Sometimes it requires some thought on my part to get the stitches off the holder onto the needle moving in the right direction. Granted, it's not much thought, but I really don't like to strain myself.

Another must-have tool is darning needles, used to darn in the ends of your yarn when you start a new skein, and to sew up the pieces of your knitting.

I've got three sizes of darning needles, and that nicely covers all yarns from lace weight to bulky. If I knitted in super-bulky yarns at a gauge of less than three stitches to the inch, I'd no doubt need another, larger needle as well. You can buy a set of two or three darning needles in a little plastic case very reasonably.

Next on the list is a tape measure. Sure, you can use a ruler in a pinch, but a tape measure is much easier to carry around, and longer, too. I've got several of them, because they mysteriously disappear in moments of need. I've got a couple of the cute little sheep tape measures, where the measuring tape comes out of, ahem, the sheep's butt, and a couple of plain vanilla ones. In a pinch, you can use all sorts of things to measure your knitting, though.

Take a plain letter-sized sheet of paper. It's 8½ by 11 inches, so there's a measuring device for you. You can fold the piece of paper in half either or both ways to measure smaller items. It's also handy (no pun intended) to know the length of your index finger (three inches for me) and the distance between outstretched tip of index finger and tip of thumb (seven inches for me). I've done many a rough measurement using just my hand.

If you are going to knit a cabled sweater, you'll want a cable needle, unless you have mastered cabling without a cable needle.

A digression here. I used a cable needle for years, until someone showed me how to make cables without a cable needle. Once I learned that, I never looked back.*

But if you prefer to use a cable needle, you'll probably need a couple. Not only are they wont to go missing, particularly if you have a cat or two, but they come in a couple of different sizes to accommodate different yarn weights. You can get straight ones (that look like a wee, tiny dpn) or bent ones. I always used bent ones because I thought they kept the stitches in line better than a straight one would, but it's really just a matter of personal preference.

One of my favorite knitting notions to collect is the stitch marker. If you are knitting a complicated pattern, it helps to mark each pattern repeat with a stitch marker, which, in its simplest manifestation, is a ring you slip on the needle between two stitches. As you knit, you just slip the marker from left to right needle when you encounter it. You can tie a bit of yarn in a color that contrasts with your working yarn and use that as a stitch marker. My favorite "utility" stitch markers are rubber rings. The rubber doesn't have the tendency to fly off the needle like some materials do. They usually come in two or three sizes to accommodate different needle sizes.

But there are many, many more fun stitch markers, such as rings with little charms and beads hanging off them. I've got markers with tiny cat beads on them, as well as ones with little bitty sheep, semiprecious stones, cartoon characters, and even some fun ones with my initials on beads. Some of these were handmade by clever friends, others purchased.

---

*There's a tutorial, with photos, on cabling without a cable needle on my website (www .wendyknits.net). Check it out!

Point protectors for your needles are also handy. These are little rubber or plastic stoppers that you pop on the pointy ends of your needles to keep the stitches from coming off when your work is picked up and shaken by an enthusiastic child or nonknitter, or when you shove everything into a tote bag. They come in all sorts of shapes and colors. I've got ones shaped like little socks and teddy bears, as well as some more austere plain ones.

You also need a knitting bag. This can be as simple as a shopping bag, though I prefer a knitting bag that has a pocket or two, because I want a place to store my knitting tools.

I'll confess that I have a knitting bag fetish. I have many, many knitting bags (at last count, over twenty), and I do actually use most of them. They are all different shapes and sizes, and each one is just right for a particular project.

And to go along with your knitting bag, you'll find a small zippered pouch handy to keep your tools in one place. The little pouches that cosmetic companies give away as promotions are, I think, the perfect size for a knitting notions bag.

So, what do I have in my knitting notions bag? Apart from some combination of the items described above, I always carry the following items:

Safety pins. I always keep a few in varying sizes. I find they are great to use as tiny stitch holders, as well as markers to show when I've completed a specified number of inches on my knitting in progress.

A pair of scissors. This pretty much goes without saying, unless you don't have a problem gnawing on your yarn with your teeth to cut it when you are scissorless. I have done this in moments of desperation, but I do not recommend it. Particularly in the company of other people. So I keep a pair of scissors in my notions bag.

A pen. Not surprisingly, my memory is not improving as I get older, so I always keep a pen handy to make notes on my pattern. A small pad of paper or Post-it notes is useful to carry as well.

A crochet hook. Crochet hooks are great for picking up dropped stitches or for working a pulled stitch over to the wrong side of the work. I keep a medium-size hook, an F or G, in my knitting notions bag.

A nail file. No matter how careful my manicure, I can't tell you how many times I've been knitting on the train and discovered a rough spot on a fingernail that catches on the yarn I'm using, on every single blessed stitch. Before it finally occurred to me to always carry a nail file with me, I was reduced, more than once, to surreptitiously gnawing at my fingernail in an attempt to file it down with my teeth. This is, no doubt, a social faux pas (and can even grow into a terrible habit that's hard to break).

Just as important to knitting as the proper tools is a good grasp of the concepts of mathematics. The knitter is not just a laborer, constructing a sweater, but an engineer, building a creation based on math. If you don't want to spend your life being a blind follower of patterns written by others, you will need to understand how a pattern is constructed. Once you can deconstruct your pattern and look at the pieces and the numbers involved, you need never fear it again.

Generally, the first thing you do when starting on a new project is to check the gauge, the number of stitches and rows it takes to comprise an inch of knitted fabric. Fear not the gauge swatch, as it is your friend!

Knitting a gauge swatch is crucial to the success of your project, particularly if you are using a yarn you've not knitted with before. A stitch or two difference between your gauge and the pattern's stated gauge can have catastrophic results. The difference of half a stitch per inch doesn't seem like much in a four-inch square, but across an entire sweater it will change the final measurements alarmingly. So knit those gauge swatches. It's best to complete a swatch of at least four inches on each side to get the more accurate measurement. The alternative to knitting gauge swatches before starting sweaters is to have a number of friends in a variety of sizes to whom you can give sweaters that don't fit you because you were not knitting to gauge.

Okay, a confession here. I don't always knit a gauge swatch. And when I do knit a gauge swatch, I almost never knit one as large as a four-inch square. This is a good example of "do as I say, not as I do."

I've been knitting forever, and I've got a pretty good idea of how different yarns will look when I knit them. I know that I tend to have a slightly looser gauge than average, so I will usually start knitting with a needle one size smaller than recommended. If I am using a new yarn, I will cast on a bit more than what I think is two inches' worth of stitches and knit for a couple of inches. But with yarn that I've used before, I will plunge right in and start knitting the sweater. I do keep a close eye on things as I knit, though, and measure as I go along. I will rip it out if I'm way off.

A lot of the types of things I knit are repetitious, though. Take Fair Isle, for example. Almost all the Fair Isle designs I have knitted are made from jumper-weight Shetland wool on US size 3 (3.25mm) needles, at a gauge of 8 stitches per inch. I know from much experience that that is my gauge for color work with that yarn and those needles. The same is true for most Norwegian designs. I am using the same yarn at the same gauge for most of them.

While most knitters can "get gauge" on the number of stitches per inch, if not with the recommended needle size, but by going up or down just a needle size or two, it's much harder to achieve both stitch gauge and row gauge simultaneously. Stitch gauge is more important. Your stitch gauge determines how big around your sweater will be. Row gauge determines the length of the sweater. Length is easily adjusted. Most patterns will tell you to knit until a piece is a certain length, a given number of inches or centimeters, rather than a certain number of rows, before you start decreasing for the armholes. Then after you complete your armhole decreases, you are told to knit until the armhole is a certain depth. You can see that you need not worry too much about your row gauge. Rather, depend on your tape measure.

When you get to the sleeves, this gets a bit trickier. Sleeves are almost always narrower at the cuff and get bigger in diameter as you go up the arm. If you are knitting from the cuff up, this increase in diameter is achieved by gradually increasing the number of stitches in the sleeve.

Say that you start with 40 stitches at the cuff after you've completed the ribbing. Your instructions tell you to increase 1 stitch at each end of every 5th row until you have 80 stitches, and then work straight until the sleeve measures seventeen inches. According to my calculations, you will need to knit 100 rows to complete the increases to get your total stitch count to 80 stitches. We'll say for this example that the cuff is two inches long, and your row gauge is 6 rows per inch. Including your two-inch cuff, your sleeve will be over 18½ inches long by the time you've reached the 100th row beyond the cuff.

To compensate for your differing row gauge, you will need to recalculate the rate of increases. If you increase a stitch at each end of every 4th row, you will complete your increases in 80 rows. Add those 80 rows (at 6 rows per inch) to the two inches of cuff and the total length of the sleeve is a bit under 15½ inches. So after you've completed your increases, you'll work straight for another inch and a half or so.

Suppose you find a pattern you adore, but the sizing is wrong. Fear not! There are a couple of ways to upsize or downsize a pattern.

One way is to cheat on the gauge. Suppose the sweater is knit at a gauge of 5 stitches to the inch. The finished circumference is 40 inches, which is 200 stitches around. If you knit at a gauge of 4.75 stitches to the inch, you'll end up with a sweater that is about 42 inches around. If you need to downsize, using smaller needles to knit at a gauge of 5.25 stitches per inch will give you a sweater that's just about 38 inches around.

I confess that I have been known to cheat in this manner. But be fore-warned: this only works for slight adjustments. A quarter of a stitch in a gauge of about 5 stitches per inch is really about as much as you should cheat; other-wise you'll end up with problems.

If you need to stick with the given gauge for your design, but want to upsize or downsize it, you'll need to rework the math for the pattern. Pattern design software can be very helpful in this undertaking, but you can do it fairly easily with just a calculator too.

If you want to add two inches to your 40-inch sweater, that's one inch in the front and one inch in the back (assuming you are knitting in pieces rather than in the round). With a gauge of 5 stitches to the inch, you would, of course, add 5 stitches each to the front and back of the sweater. If you need to have an even number of stitches for pattern reasons, add 6 stitches.

If your design has drop shoulders, all you have to worry about is incorpo-rating those extra stitches into the pattern when you are working the neck shaping. You will have to decide if the extra inch will fall on either side of the neck, or if you want to make a wider neck, or perhaps a little of both. For a set-in or raglan sleeve design, consider decreasing extra stitches at the start of the armhole shaping to compensate for the additional stitches you add.

Resizing a design with a set pattern that repeats is a bit more challenging. You need to add stitches in multiples that can be incorporated into your stitch pattern, or in partial repeats of the pattern, if that is appropriate. If you are doing a texture stitch that has a ten-stitch repeat, for example, you could add a partial repeat at either side of the piece. But if you are knitting lace, partial repeats might not work, depending upon your lace stitch. You may only be able to add full repeats.

For a Fair Isle design knitted in the round, you can only add full pattern repeats, unless you don't mind having the pattern look a bit odd at the sides where you would have the partial repeats. You do need to be careful when adding pattern repeats to a Fair Isle. You want to make sure that you keep the pattern centered properly.

I've had some success adjusting Arans, particularly with those that alternate a cable panel with a panel of a background stitch. While you would definitely have problems expanding a cable, you can easily add stitches to a moss stitch or reverse stockinette background.

The bottom line in this is that you are the boss. If there's something you don't like about a design, change it! I very rarely knit anything exactly according to the pattern. Consider this: a pattern may be made by a wide variety of women, ranging in height from five feet to six feet. A five-foot-tall woman will almost certainly want to make her sweater shorter than the six-foot-tall woman.

The length of a design will often vary according to the size—the larger the circumference of the sweater, the longer it is. But you should look at this as a guideline only. Once again, measuring a sweater you own that fits you well is a good idea. Check the length to the armhole and the total length of the sweater to help you decide how long to knit the pattern.

I am five feet six inches tall, which, I believe, is considered average. However, I have slightly shorter than average arms, so I almost always knit my sleeves an inch or so shorter than the pattern directs. I have a knitting friend who has slightly longer than average arms, so she always adds an inch or so. Lately I've made several sweaters that have sleeves that are designed to reach almost to one's knuckles. While this may look pretty, I find it impractical for everyday wear, so I take this into consideration as well when altering a pattern to suit me. Remember, also, to take these sorts of adjustments into consideration when buying your yarn for your project.

Another alteration I often make is to the neckband or collar of a pattern. I wish I had a lovely long swanlike neck, but the reality is that I don't. I have a short stubby neck. I look ridiculous in turtlenecks—like a frightened turtle, actually. I may find a pattern that I like that has a turtleneck and knit it. But I will invariably knit it with a crew neck instead.

I am also not a huge fan of the roll neck, so I'll substitute a crew neck for a roll neck every time. Conversely, if you like a roll neck, you can use that in place of a crew neck.

The same goes for the hem of a sweater. I don't like roll hems, so I will substitute ribbing, or a stockinette hem with a facing, or maybe a garter stitch or seed stitch edge on the bottom of my sweater. Which one I use depends on the look I want for the finished sweater.

Armed with your sweater design software, a library of patterns that fit and appeal to you, and your calculator, you can go forth and conquer almost any knitting pattern you find!

Chapter 9 • What Was I Thinking?

I LOVE TO DESIGN SWEATERS. There is something enormously satisfying about creating something and taking it from idea to sketches to pattern to knitted pieces to completed sweater.

Insomnia plays a large part in the design process for me. Sometimes I lie awake half the night, thinking about the things one usually thinks of when one can't sleep. But as I doze off, I have yarn dreams. Knitted swatches invade my mind. Fat plaited cables and diamond patterns elbow gloriously colored snippets of Fair Isle out of the way. I'm pretty sure I can see a beefy Celtic knot punch a Fair Isle swatch right in the peerie. And the lace! Lots and lots of lace! The lace swatches hang back uncertainly at first, afraid of the macho cables and aggressive brightly colored Fair Isles. Slowly, though, they approach. Eyelets on a stockinette background, feather and fan, picot edgings. All these swatches are climbing over each other, jockeying for position. Then I hear them.

"Knit me!"

"No, knit *me* first!"

"You have the perfect yarn for *me*!"

So I wake up with a jump. Then I lie awake until the alarm goes off, thinking about swatches and patterns and design possibilities.

It's not easy having voices in your head. Particularly when you feel compelled to do what they tell you. Fortunately for everyone, my voices are telling me to knit.

How did I become a "knitting designer"? Am I a knitting designer? What makes you a knitting designer? My opinion is that if you think about what you are knitting and look for ways to modify and change patterns to suit you, you are well on the way. For me, it was an evolutionary process.

I'm always changing patterns. For example:

"What are you knitting?" someone will ask.

"Oh, it's this pattern in this magazine. But I don't like the roll neck so I'm making a crew neck. And I don't like the bottom edge so I'm changing the ribbing. And I'm making the sleeves a bit wider and shorter."

This is my modus operandi: to change the pattern until it suits me. And I know lots and lots of other people who do this too.

The first time I designed a whole sweater, almost twenty years ago, I did so because the yarn spoke to me. I have no memory (now there's a surprise) of where or how I acquired it, but a lovely bulky-weight, slightly fuzzy, olive green wool came into my possession. I do remember that it came from Sweden and the color had a rustic hand-dyed look.

When I looked at the yarn, I knew immediately what it wanted to be: a cropped pullover with a square neck, long sleeves, and pockets. I knitted a tiny gauge swatch, did some calculations, and dived right in. I didn't write down what I did, because I could remember for the length of time it took me to finish the sweater what I actually was doing. I could successfully keep the number of stitches, the length I knitted to, and so on, in my head. These days, my short-term memory is not what it used to be. I can memorize complicated charts and retain them for years, but I can't remember from one sleeve to the next how many rows I have knitted or how many increases I have done, so I have finally learned to write everything down.

The olive green sweater actually came out pretty well, and I loved it. I still have it, though I haven't worn it for years. The pants that it matched perfectly are long gone. Outgrown, no doubt.

My next designing attempt was my Pink Floyd sweater. I knitted a sweater depicting the album cover of *Dark Side of the Moon*. For the uninitiated, the cover art depicts a white beam of light hitting a prism and refracting into a rainbow against a black background.

I got out my graph paper and colored pencils and charted out the design, which was relatively easily done. It was also easy to find yarn in the proper colors: black, gray-white, and the colors of the rainbow. I bought a worsted-weight wool/mohair blend that was available in all the colors I needed.

I knitted a crewneck long-sleeved pullover, with the front of the album worked on the front of the sweater, and the back of the album on the back of the sweater, done in intarsia.

And then, because I liked it so much, I reworked the pattern for sport-weight cotton and made a short-sleeved version. This time, I knitted a plain black sweater and when the knitting was done, worked all the colors in duplicate stitch. The results were surprisingly good, and I still have that short-sleeved version. The long-sleeved one has been lost in the mists of time. I sure used to get a heck of a lot of attention at Pink Floyd concerts when I wore one of my *Dark Side* sweaters. And a lot of interesting offers. Some of them had something to do with knitting sweaters. Some did not.

In the intervening years I knitted a lot of Fair Isles and Arans, and occasionally created a design of my own.

Shortly after I entered the world of knit blogging, some readers of my blog expressed interest in learning how to knit Fair Isle. I asked if anyone was interested in a group project to knit a simple Fair Isle design. Several people expressed interest, so the Fearless Fair Isle project was born. I designed a slightly cropped pullover with a crew neck and dropped shoulders and ribbing around the bottom. It was designed for two sizes: 42" and 45½" around. The design used a total of seven colors and I worked out three different colorways and created charts for the pattern, using a computer program for designing stitch and color patterns. The recommended yarn for this project was the traditional yarn for Fair Isles: jumper-weight Shetland wool (roughly equivalent to fingering weight).

A couple hundred people, located all across the United States, and even a few in Europe, communicated via an online group set up at Yahoo! Groups, and we went through the process of deciding on colors, knitting swatches to figure out our gauges, and discussing the techniques for two-color knitting. As most of the group members purchased their yarn from the same source, a supplier in Scotland, we conjectured that they were probably wondering why a number of people were suddenly purchasing the same combination of colors. At least one member made her design from cotton rather than wool, so we had some discussions about structuring a Fair Isle knitted in cotton.

Although at the time I lived in abject terror that my design was flawed and I was wasting everyone's time, I think the project was a great success. Several of the members posted photos of their completed Fair Isles. And as far as I know, my pattern didn't stink too badly. Or if it did, everyone was too kind to bring it up, so the pattern is still available on my website.

After we completed the Fearless Fair Isle project, there was talk of a follow-up "Aggressive Aran" or "Go-for-It Gansey" project, but I never got either of those projects going. I just wasn't feeling any inspiration at the time.

Sometimes I find a successful design springs unexpectedly from something else entirely. Recently I started knitting a sweater from my own handspun wool. What I had in mind was a plain pullover with a simple lace border around the hem and the sleeves. I started out knitting a feather and fan pattern as the border. Eight inches into the back of the sweater, I ripped it out because I didn't like the way it looked.

This was one of those defining moments for me, given my hatred of ripping out. That I let the piece grow to eight inches before ripping is testament to my ability to convince myself that although the thing looked heinous, it would turn out okay.

Although I had actually done a gauge swatch, I finally let myself see that I was not happy with the way the knitted fabric looked. And I didn't like the way the feather and fan pattern looked in the heavy-weight handspun yarn—it was far too fussy.

I started over at a different gauge, with a different, simpler lace pattern (the one called vine lace that I used in chapter 2's Vince sweater). I worked eight rows of the border and went to bed.

I dreamed about vine lace all night. And I woke up far too early the next morning (sadly, a Saturday) with my head full of it. Half awake, only partially conscious, I thought about my vine lace dreams. Then I started thinking about vines. Then grapevines specifically. Then grapes.

You know how your mind starts racing when you are trying desperately to clear it of all thoughts so you can fall back asleep? Clearing my cluttered mind almost never works, and it didn't this time. I resigned myself to an endless loop of knitting thoughts and soon an idea for a new design popped out and presented itself to me. I could see a large triangular shawl with a grapevine theme. The top part of the shawl would have a lace pattern that looked like little bunches of grapes. I'd do a deep border of vine lace, then edge it with an edging that looked like leaves. As this point I was already calling it my Grape Arbor Shawl.

I got up and went in the stash room in search of yarn for my shawl. Having an obscenely large stash paid off: I found the perfect yarn in minutes. I had

1,000 yards of a DK-weight 100% silk yarn, hand-dyed in lavender and green. Perfect!

I started up my laptop and charted the "Bunches of Grapes" pattern. I knitted a couple of swatches with the silk yarn and decided on a needle size. I was set to go. I abandoned the poor handspun sweater and worked feverishly on the Grape Arbor Shawl for the next ten days or so, until it was complete. Fortunately, I had the sense to take copious notes, so I was later able to write out the pattern (which you will find beginning on page 157).

Then I returned to the handspun sweater and completed it. I even managed to document the design process so that I was able to write out that pattern as well.

This was a prolific couple of months for me. It was a dreary winter, and it seemed as though the lack of color and warmth outside was directly proportional to the many ideas I had for knitting designs.

Having a creative (if somewhat disorderly) mind has advantages when I pick out patterns by others that I want to knit. There are certain patterns that jump out and scream "Knit me!" What makes them do that? What are the design elements that capture my attention and spark my imagination?

To my way of thinking, there's nothing like a carefully thought out, well-designed sweater. Loving Aran sweaters as I do, I am extraordinarily picky about the Arans I knit. Aran sweaters are made up of a number of different design elements. If one motif seems a bit off to me, if it doesn't seem to go with the other motifs, the whole design is ruined for me.

The same goes for Fair Isles. The colors, of course, have to live side by side happily and in harmony or I'm not interested. Actually, a lot of Fair Isles don't appeal to me, particularly the older designs based on museum pieces. The colors are often too bright and jarring, such as brick red and mustard yellow side by side with brown and black. I much prefer the softer, more harmonious combinations that some contemporary Fair Isle designers put together. I am particularly drawn to designs inspired by nature: a field of flowers or rocks on a beach.

But it's not just the colors. The motifs have to be perfect (perfect for me, that is) or I'm just not interested. I recently realized that abstract designs in Fair Isle are a turn-off for me. Make those babies nicely geometric and symmetrical, please!

Too often, magazines and books of knitting patterns are put together by photo stylists who, I'm sorry, have no idea what a knitter wants to see when looking at the publication. We don't want dramatic or busy backgrounds. We don't want artsy poses and airbrushing. We want to see the sweater.

A beautiful—or badly flawed—design can be obscured by fashion photography. The photo accompanying a pattern may feature a lovely model who is striking an odd pose or is photographed at an odd angle. I recall seeing a pattern for a bulky pullover sweater that featured two women wearing these bulky pullovers over bathing suits, tossing a beach ball between them. You have to train yourself to look past the smoke and mirrors to be able to see what the design really looks like. You have to learn how to recognize photography tricks that are used to camouflage poorly designed, ill-fitting garments. And conversely, you must look past horrific yarn choices and bilious colors to recognize the beauty of a design.

If the neckline of a sweater is obscured by a scarf in the photo, that's a red flag. I always assume there's something wrong with the neck of the garment. Why else would they feel the need to hide it? If the model is striking a bizarre pose, scrutinize the photo carefully to see if there's something odd about the design that they're trying to camouflage. I am suspicious by nature. I always suspect the worst.

And another problem is that the design is usually photographed on a model who, on a fat day, weighs ninety pounds. The same sweater on a normal-sized person can look very different.

Hopefully the publication will include schematic drawings of the designs. I always find them to be my best bet for figuring out what is actually going on in the sweater. You can see the basic shape, size, and length of the sweater by scrutinizing the schematic.

Even if there is no schematic included with the pattern, you can sketch one out on graph paper based on the pattern. You can tell the length and width, and the proportions of the sleeves, from reading the pattern directions, and do a rough sketch from that. Your sketch, along with whatever photo of the design is offered, can give you a pretty good idea of what the design actually looks like.

Color and yarn choice can also hugely influence how much you like a design. When I'm thumbing through a knitting magazine, I'll often skip over designs photographed in colors I don't like (especially yellow). It's a bad habit. Because often, if I stop and use my imagination to picture the sweater knitted in a color I like, the pattern's good points will reveal themselves to me.

The same is true of yarn. A plain sweater that looks boring in a smooth worsted can be fabulous in, say, a tweed yarn. And vice versa: a cabled sweater in a textured yarn can look too busy, but the same sweater knitted in smooth worsted can be truly lovely. You need to train your eye to separate the wheat from the chaff and also unearth those diamonds in the rough or just use them to inspire your own creations.

The following is one of my favorites from among my original designs: my Lucy sweater, a short-sleeved pullover with gentle waist shaping and a lace border on the hem and sleeves. This is one of those projects in which I actually had the foresight to document the design process from start to finish while developing it, making it much easier for me to write out the pattern.

Lucy Top

Finished Measurements

35 (39, 42½, 46)" chest
19 (19, 20, 20)" length

Materials

4 (5, 6, 6) skeins Rowan Calmer (75% cotton, 25% microfiber, 175yd/50g skein)
US size 5 (3.75mm) 24" circular needle (or size to get gauge)

Gauge

24 sts and 28 rows = 4" measured over stockinette stitch using size 5 needle

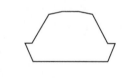

19 (19, 20, 20)"

17½ (19½, 21¼, 23)"

Lace Pattern Chart

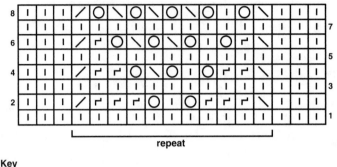

Key

I	Knit (k) on right side, purl (p) on wrong side
⌐	Knit through back loop (k tbl)
\	Slip 2 stitches as if to knit, knit those 2 stitches together (ssk)
/	Knit 2 together (k2tog)
O	Yarn over (yo)

Lace Pattern in Words

Row 1 (WS) and all other WS rows: Purl across.

Row 2: K3, *ssk, (k1tbl) 3 times, yo, k1, yo, (k1tbl) 3 times, k2tog; repeat from * until 3 sts remain, k3.

Row 4: K3, *ssk, (k1tbl) 2 times, yo, k1, yo, ssk, yo, (k1tbl) 2 times, k2tog; repeat from * until 3 sts remain, k3.

Row 6: K3, *ssk, k1tbl, yo, k1, (yo, ssk) 2 times, yo, k1tbl, k2tog; repeat from * until 3 sts remain, k3.

Row 8: K3, *ssk, yo, k1, (yo, ssk) 3 times, yo, k2tog; repeat from * until 3 sts remain, k3.

Directions

Except for the neckband, you will work the pieces for this sweater back and forth on the circular needle.

Back

Cast on 105 (116, 127, 138) stitches.

Knit 4 rows.

Work two repeats (a total of 16 rows) of lace pattern.

Work in stockinette stitch for 9 (9, 11, 11) rows, starting with a wrong side (purl) row.

Shape waist:

Decrease 1 stitch at each end of the next row, then on every other row 8 times more—87 (98, 109, 120) sts.

Work 9 (9, 11, 11) rows even.

Increase 1 stitch at each end of the next row, then every 4th row 8 times more—105 (116, 127, 138) sts.

Note: If you prefer, you can knit this design without the waist shaping to make a sweater with a boxier silhouette. You can also increase or decrease the amount of waist shaping to suit the figure of the wearer.

Work even until piece measures 11½ (11½, 12, 12)" from the beginning, end with a WS row.

Shape armholes:

Bind off 6 sts at the beginning of the next 2 rows, 2 sts at the beginning of the next 4 rows. Decrease 1 st at each end of the next row, then every 4th row twice, then every 6th row twice—75 (86, 97, 108) sts.

Work even until armhole measures 7½ (7½, 8, 8)", end with a WS row.

Shape neck:

Work across 26 (31, 36, 42) sts, attach another ball of yarn and bind off center 23 (24, 25, 24) sts, work remaining 26 (31, 36, 42) sts.

Work both sides simultaneously on separate yarn balls.

At each neck edge, bind off 5 stitches once, 2 sts once, and 1 st once. Place the remaining 18 (23, 28, 34) sts for each shoulder on stitch holders.

Front

Work as for back until armhole measures 6 (6, 6½, 6½)", end with a WS row.

Shape neck:

Work 31 (36, 41, 47) sts, attach another ball of yarn and bind off center 13 (14, 15, 14) sts, work remaining 31 (36, 41, 47) sts.

Work both sides simultaneously.

At each neck edge, bind off 3 sts once, 2 sts twice, and 1 st 6 times.

Work until armhole depth matches the back.

Place the remaining 18 (23, 28, 34) sts for each shoulder on stitch holders.

Sleeves

Cast on 83 stitches.

Knit 4 rows.

Work a total of 16 rows of lace pattern, then work in stockinette stitch for 11 rows, starting with a wrong side (purl) row.

At the same time, increase (working increase in stockinette stitch at each end and keeping lace pattern correct) 1 st at each end of every 4th row 4 (4, 6, 6) times—91 (91, 95, 95) sts.

Work until the piece measures 3½", ending with a wrong side row.

Shape cap:

Bind off 6 sts at the beginning of the next 2 rows, 3 sts at the beginning of the next 6 rows. Dec 1 st at each end of the next row, then every other row 15 times more. Work 1 row even. Bind off 2 sts at the beginning of the next 8 rows. Bind off remaining 13 (13, 17, 17) sts.

Join Front and Back

Graft front and back shoulders together or work three-needle bind-off.

Neckband

Pick up 6 stitches per inch knitwise evenly around the neck, join and work in the round as follows:

Row 1: Purl 1 round.

Row 2: Knit 1 round.

Row 3: Bind off knitwise.

Set in sleeves and sew up sleeve and side seams.

As I said, sometimes I look at a yarn and know exactly what to make from it. The Melody sweater is a perfect example of a yarn speaking to me to let me know what it wants to become. I came across the Blue Sky Organic Cotton in my local yarn shop. It's a lovely soft worsted-weight cotton in several natural shades. I immediately thought of a boxy cabled pullover.

Why the name Melody? Because I was knitting along on it, thinking about the cables looking like chains, and that got "Unchained Melody" running through my head, and well . . . one thing led to another. Of course, to most people the cables look more like little fishies set end to end, which just reinforces my opinion that I have a slightly skewed view of things.

Melody Cabled Pullover

Finished Measurements

42 (44, 46)" chest
24" length

Materials

7 (8, 9) skeins Blue Sky Organic Cotton (100% cotton, 150yd/100g skein)
US size 7 (4.5mm) straight needles
US 7 16" circular needle
Cable needle

Gauge

16 sts and 20 rows = 4", measured over stockinette stitch using size 7 needles

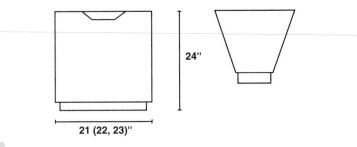

24"

21 (22, 23)"

Cable Pattern Chart

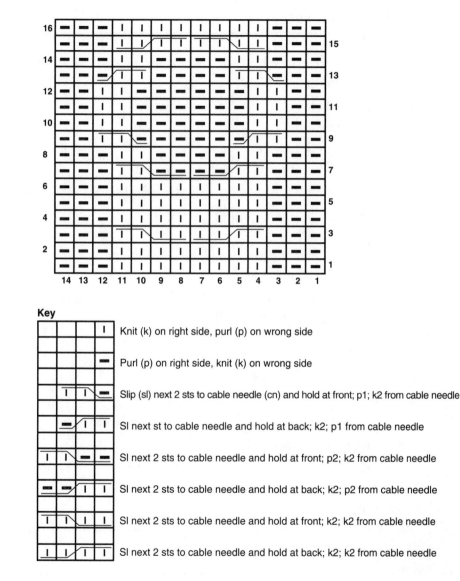

Key

			I	Knit (k) on right side, purl (p) on wrong side
			▬	Purl (p) on right side, knit (k) on wrong side
	I	I	▬	Slip (sl) next 2 sts to cable needle (cn) and hold at front; p1; k2 from cable needle
	▬	I	I	Sl next st to cable needle and hold at back; k2; p1 from cable needle
I	I	▬	▬	Sl next 2 sts to cable needle and hold at front; p2; k2 from cable needle
▬	▬	I	I	Sl next 2 sts to cable needle and hold at back; k2; p2 from cable needle
I	I	I	I	Sl next 2 sts to cable needle and hold at front; k2; k2 from cable needle
I	I	I	I	Sl next 2 sts to cable needle and hold at back; k2; k2 from cable needle

Cable Pattern in Words

(Worked over 14 stitches and 16 rows)

Row 1 (RS): P3, k8, p3.

Row 2 and all even rows: Knit the knit stitches and purl the purl stitches.

Row 3: P3, (sl next 2 sts to cn and hold at back, k2, k2 from cn), (sl next 2 sts to cn and hold at front, k2, k2 from cn), p3.

Row 5: As row 1.

Row 7: P3, (sl next 2 sts to cn and hold at back, k2, p2 from cn), (sl next 2 sts to cn and hold at front, p2, k2 from cn), p3.

Row 9: P2, (sl next st to cn and hold at back, k2, p1 from cn), p4, (sl next 2 sts to cn and hold at front, p1, k2 from cn), p2.

Row 11: P2, k2, p6, k2, p2.

Row 13: P2, (sl next 2 sts to cn and hold at front, p1, k2 from cn), p4, (sl next st to cn and hold at back, k2, p1 from cn), p2.

Row 15: P3, (sl next 2 sts to cn and hold at front, k2, k2 from cn), (sl next 2 sts to cn and hold at back, k2, k2 from cn), p3.

Directions

Back

With straight needles, cast on 91 (95, 99) stitches.

Create seed stitch over 5 rows, by working each row as follows: (k1, p1) to last st, end with k1.

Next row (WS): Increase 7 stitches evenly across the row—98 (102, 106) stitches.

Begin cable pattern:

Row 1 (RS): *K14 (15, 16), work row 1 of cable pattern over next 14 stitches; repeat from * twice more; k14 (15, 16).

Row 2: *P14 (15, 16), work row 2 of cable pattern over next 14 stitches; repeat from * twice more; p14 (15, 16).

Continue in this manner until all 16 rows of the cable pattern have been worked, then repeat until you have completed row 2 of the 8th repeat of the cable pattern, or until your work measures 23".

Shape the back neck:

Continuing to follow the cable pattern as established, work across 34 (36, 38) stitches. Turn and work on these stitches only.

Bind off 2 stitches at the beginning of every other row 3 times, then place the remaining 28 (30, 32) stitches on a holder.

Place the center 30 stitches on a holder for the back neck, then work the remaining stitches to correspond to the first side.

Front

Work as for back until you have completed 6 cable repeats, or to 20½".

Shape the front neck:

Continuing to follow the cable pattern as established, work across 39 (41, 43) stitches. Turn and work on these stitches only.

Cast off 2 stitches at the beginning of every other row 3 times, then decrease 1 stitch at the neck edge every other row until 28 (30, 32) stitches remain. Work to correspond to the back in length, and place the remaining stitches on a holder.

Place the center 20 stitches on a holder for the front neck, then work the remaining stitches to correspond to the first side.

Join Front and Back

Join the front and back pieces at the shoulders using a three-needle bind-off.

Neckband

Using 16" circular needle and starting at the right shoulder seam, pick up and knit 7 stitches down the right back neck, knit the 30 stitches from the holder for the center back neck, pick up and knit 7 stitches for left back neck, pick up and knit 15 stitches for left front neck, knit the 20 stitches from the holder, then pick up and knit 15 stitches for right front neck—94 stitches. Join and work in the round in seed stitch (k1, p1) for 5 rounds, then cast off in seed stitch.

Sleeves

With straight needles, cast on 39 stitches. Work seed stitch for 5 rows as follows: (k1, p1) to last stitch, end with k1. On last row, increase 1 stitch—40 stitches.

Begin cable pattern:

Row 1 (RS): *Knit 13, work row 1 of cable pattern over next 14 stitches, knit 13.

Row 2: *Purl 13, work row 2 of cable pattern over next 14 stitches, purl 13.

Continue in pattern, and increase 1 stitch at each end of every 4th row, until there is a total of 80 stitches.

Work even until the sleeve measures 16½", or desired length. Bind off.

Finishing

Measure down 9" on each side from the shoulder seam and sew each sleeve to the body. Sew sleeve and side seams.

Chapter 10 • The Fiber Snob

MY NAME IS WENDY AND I AM A FIBER SNOB.

What is a fiber snob? To my way of thinking, a fiber snob is someone who revels in the glory that is luxury fiber. It is someone who eschews cheap acrylic and cotton that can be purchased at the dime store.

No doubt I am dating myself, using the phrase "dime store." But that's what we used to have when I was a kid. And in the crafts department of the dime store, you could buy huge skeins of knitting worsted-weight acrylic that often came in colors that would give nightmares to a clown. I remember seeing skeins labeled "2 full pounds for 99 cents!" Like that was a good thing.

Okay, does anyone remember the ombre yarn of the 1970s? I recently did a Google search on the Internet and got 7,330 hits on the search term "ombre yarn." So clearly, it still exists.

For the uninitiated (and I'm unsure whether to pity or envy you), ombre yarn is yarn that is dyed in multiple colors. Generally, the yarn will be dyed in multiple shades of the same color or in different colors that may—or more often may not—complement each other. The yarn color changes every couple of inches or so. "Ombre" means "shade" in French, so it does make some sort of sense.

Please note that I am not talking about the delightful variegated hand-painted yarns that today are becoming more and more popular. These small masterpieces usually start with a high-quality "base yarn" and are lovingly painted by an artist. Someone with color sense.

In the 1970s, my grandmother crocheted a very funky granny-square vest for me out of ombre yarn, in shades of brown and orange, thank you very much. I loved that vest and wore it every chance I got. I was groovy. I was beyond cool. In my defense, I was also fourteen.

This is exactly the type of ombre yarn that I now fear . . . and loathe.

Years ago, a friend of mine decided she wanted to take up knitting. This was no doubt due to my influence, as I carried my big bag o' knitting wherever I went. Because she wasn't sure if she was going to master or enjoy knitting, she didn't want to invest a lot of money in the yarn. This was a completely reasonable plan, right?

Said friend purchased a pattern to make a simple boatneck sweater. She then purchased a quantity of ombre acrylic yarn.

(Insert ominous music here.)

Let me pause here to say that there are some ombre yarns that are quite nice, and look lovely knitted up into, say, a baby blanket. Sadly, this ombre yarn was not of that genre. Not only was the ombre dyeing done in a bizarre mishmash of colors, the yarn itself was of poor quality. You know the type: it had a harsh, plasticky feel to it, and I swear it formed pills just by you looking at it. If one were to set fire to it (and I swear to you here that I have never done that) it melts.

But all the same, Friend optimistically knitted the ombre yarn into the sweater, even though it was obvious from the start that the resulting sweater was going to be the Ugliest Sweater on the Face of the Earth. Bar none. Friend bravely soldiered on, thinking, I guess, that everything would work out for the best and the ugly sweater pieces would magically be transformed into a beautiful finished object. (We've all been there.)

But sadly, the ombre pieces, when sewn together into the ombre sweater, did not transform themselves into a thing of beauty. It was hands down the ugliest sweater I have ever seen. Friend agreed with me. Friend was devastated. Friend never knitted again. Friend did send the sweater off to a refugee relief project, but only after some soul-searching. She said she felt bad about sending such an ugly sweater to someone who was already having a rough go of it.

The moral of the story? Never knit with cheap, ugly yarn. It will suck the soul out of you.

Ask me how I know.

I was young once. And when you are a teenager addicted to knitting and cheap acrylic is all you can afford, cheap acrylic is what you will use. Some cheap acrylic is actually quite acceptable to knit. It does have its place. If you are looking for something that will wear well after being machine-washed a billion times, go for the acrylic. Or an acrylic/wool blend. If you are knitting something for a child who will outgrow the item in a nanosecond, it's worth thinking about soft, well-made acrylic. If you are knitting blankets to be put in the cages in animal shelters, since these will be washed in commercial machines, go with acrylic all the way!

And if you are strapped for money (and I've been in that situation more times than I care to remember), you make do. Once, during lean times, I knitted a lovely textured design from acrylic yarn purchased at a craft store. I once knitted my brother an Aran sweater from an acrylic similarly acquired. But the sad truth is that while I was knitting beautiful designs in cheap acrylic, my heart ached.

At the moment I am solvent. So here's my plan: I am stockpiling fine yarns against future catastrophes in my aforementioned stash. (How does one build a stash? In one easy lesson: buy yarn. No, please—no need to thank me for this pearl of wisdom.)

I used to buy yarn one project at a time. This was back in the days of going to the yarn shop and picking out yarn for a project, or mail-ordering yarn for a project from a catalog. Now there are so many more temptations out there.

Online auctions are right up there in my top temptations. There is so much yarn to be had, some of it at discount prices. I see an auction for ten skeins of a gorgeous silk ribbon yarn in my favorite shade of green . . . obviously, I gotta buy it! The next day, the same seller has the same yarn for sale, but in chocolate brown. Chocolate brown, I tell you! Obviously, I can't live without that. Click. It's mine. When I buy, say, thirty-odd skeins of pink silk/cotton blend yarn, I rarely have any idea what I'm going to make with it, but I just can't bear the idea of someone else getting them.

Such are the traps of the online auction. Now add to that the countless online stores that you can access twenty-four hours a day, seven days a week (Do you suffer from insomnia? Get online and order yarn!) and you'll have an admirable stash in no time at all. Note that you need to be cautious when buying yarn online, as colors seen on the computer monitor can look very different in real life.

The most evil of the online stores are the ones that sell discontinued yarn at a discount. At these places, the sense of urgency is quite real. If you don't jump on a hot deal right away, someone else will. And you may never see that yarn again. It could vanish from the earth. . . .

But the most satisfying yarn-acquisition experience by far is the trip to the local yarn shop. No matter how spiffy your computer monitor, no matter the bells and whistles on your system, nothing beats seeing and fondling yarn in person.

And I have noted that I buy more yarn when I can get up close and personal with it.

I love to visit my local yarn shop, Knit Happens, when it's just received a shipment of something new. Pristine bags of yarn come tumbling out of the big cardboard shipping boxes in an elegant rainbow of colors. It's more than an addicted knitter can resist. I am weak. I love to pick out yarns and line the skeins up like little soldiers on the table. I put like colors together, and then I separate them. I pile them in little pyramids, and then I stand them on end.

That said, I do get a thrill when I receive yarn in the mail. Ripping into the packaging feels like Christmas morning to me. With the first glimpse of the yarn, I feel a heady rush. If the yarn is packaged in a plastic bag, I always open the bag and pull out a skein to fondle.

The yarn sits out for a while, before it gets filed away in the stash room. I can't quite bear to have it out of my line of vision until I've had a chance to enjoy it for a while.

So, we've established that I've got masses and masses of lovely yarn. But what really sets my fingertips a-tingling is luxury yarn. I love cashmere. I love silk. I love merino wool.

And what is the most luxurious of luxury yarn? I can answer that.

Qiviut. Can we have a moment of silence, please?

Qiviut (pronounced KEE-vee-ut; and sometimes called "qiviuk") is the extraordinarily fine and soft undercoat of the arctic musk ox. Qiviut is reputedly eight times warmer than sheep's wool and is finer than cashmere. Apparently musk oxen are few and far between, because qiviut production is extremely limited. Most, if not all, of the qiviut I've seen comes from Alaska or Canada.

I don't remember when I first learned about qiviut. It was in those long-ago pre-Internet days. I most likely read about it in a knitting magazine. I do remember that I mail-ordered a small quantity of fingering-weight qiviut from an ad in a knitting magazine. When it arrived, I reveled in the glory that is qiviut. It was a warm light brown, its natural color, and hands down the softest fiber I've ever had the privilege of fondling.

I knitted a hat from that qiviut. Not one of my smarter moves, as I wear a hat maybe once every three years. And I hang my head in shame when I report that I never once wore the qiviut hat. But I did take the poor hat out of the drawer periodically and play with it.

Years later, a friend gave me an ounce of lace-weight qiviut as a birthday gift. I ordered a second ounce from the same source (now apparently out of business—its website has vanished) and made a lace scarf.

This little gem gets plenty of wear. It is warm, but incredibly light, and oh, did I mention the softness? Divine. Whenever I wear it I insist that people touch it, so that they, too, will know the glory that is qiviut. People I know, that is. I am not quite to the point of demanding that strangers fondle my qiviut. But it's close at hand.

It occurred to me recently that I really ought to do something with the qiviut that I had knitted into a hat.

I think you should know that up to this point, I had never, ever ripped out a fully knitted item to reuse the yarn. Nor had I even contemplated it. But here I was, thinking about doing just that. Such is the power of qiviut.

I carefully ripped out the hat, skeined the yarn on my swift (an umbrella-like contraption that holds a skein of yarn while you wind it into a ball), washed it and weighted it to get the kinks out of it, and hung it up to dry.

I had 200 yards of wonderful, glorious qiviut. What to make from it? I already had a qiviut scarf. Another qiviut hat was not to be considered, given the history of the previous qiviut hat, now disassembled.

Enter my friend Johanne, who lives in Sweden.

Our e-mails to each other are full of talk about—what else?—yarn. She has jokingly mentioned on several occasions that she doesn't quite believe that there is such a thing as qiviut, that I am making it up, just to mess with her. Although that does sound like something I would do, I always assure her that this is not the case.

We had some discussion about what my reclaimed qiviut should become. Johanne's suggestion was a pair of beaded pulse warmers. Johanne makes beautiful beaded pulse warmers. I know this firsthand, as she sent me a lovely pair as a gift.

What a perfect use for a luxury fiber! I love fingerless gloves and pulse warmers. They provide a surprising measure of warmth while allowing you to keep your fingers free for tasks that require digital dexterity (like knitting). My office is usually quite chilly in the winter, so I make good use of these items.

Not only did Johanne come up with an excellent use for my qiviut, but she volunteered to knit my qiviut pulse warmers for me. Would anyone like to place a bet about how quickly I got my qiviut in the mail to her?

The rewards for this action are twofold. First, I get someone else to knit the beaded pulse warmers for me. And not just anyone: someone who will do so beautifully.

Second, I force Johanne to knit with qiviut. And because there is enough qiviut for two pairs of pulse warmers, I have insisted she knit a pair for herself as well. She may never be the same again.

At this point, I need to confess to you the Incident of the Koigu.

Koigu KPPPM is a lovely fingering-weight merino wool that is hand-painted in beautiful variegated tones. Koigu is so not ombre. It is the anti-ombre. It is heavenly. A gateway drug, if you will, for burgeoning fiber snobs. Apart from the variegated Koigu, there are also "nearly monochrome" colorways: solid colors with some subtle shading. I knitted a lace shawl from the nearly monochrome black Koigu, and it is nothing short of glorious.

At one point Johanne was searching for a fingering-weight yarn that would work for a design she wanted to knit. As I have knitted many sweaters in fingering weight and had lots of leftovers, I put together a few samples to send her, and in a fit of evil genius, slipped some Koigu in with it.

The poor woman has not been the same since. Koigu is not easily obtainable in Sweden, where she lives.

This is the ultimate in fiber snob enabling. I managed to expose a friend to the glory that is Koigu and ensure that she become obsessed with it because of its limited availability to her. Clearly, my work here should have been done.

Do I have much Koigu in my stash? You bet I do. I've got ten skeins each of several colorways, and two skeins each of several more. I am hesitant to use it only because when I use it, it will be gone. I did break down and knit a pair of gloves from one of my two-skein lots, but immediately after doing so, experienced a panic attack, because I had slightly depleted my Koigu stash without replacing the used skeins. It's just so darned pretty that most of the time I'd rather look at it than knit it. The skeins are like little jewels, nestled together. They glow.

If the knitted item is for someone else, however, it is okay to dip into your stash of precious yarns. Don't ask me why this is true. It just is. Hey, it's my rule and I don't need a rational reason for it. A while back I had three skeins of Koigu in shades of gold and brown. It was not relegated to the stash room. It was dangling seductively out of a basket in my living room. At the time I was participating in an online knitting secret pals program, and found out that my secret pal loved these colors. So I knitted her a lace scarf from my Koigu without a second thought. And I enjoyed every second of the knitting. Like I said, if it's for someone else, dipping into the stash of fine, fine yarns is perfectly fine.

My rules may not make any sense. But they work for me.

Once in a great while, I buy a luxury fiber that goes on the needles, rather than into the stash. The silk I used to knit the Lauren sweater is such a fiber: Alchemy Silk Purse.

The Lauren sweater is a simple V-neck tank, and the silk I used to knit it is downright sinful. But the good news is that it takes very little yarn, so you can justify splurging for a decadent silk yarn. I made mine in a lovely acid green. You could, of course, substitute a less expensive yarn. But why would you want to?

Lauren Tank

Finished Measurements

34½ (38, 41½, 45)" chest
20½ (20½, 21½, 22)" length

Materials

4 (4, 5, 6) skeins Alchemy Silk Purse (100% silk, 138yd/50g skein)
US size 5 (3.75mm) and size 6 (4mm) circular needles

Gauge

22 sts and 24 rows = 4" measured over stockinette stitch using size 6 needle

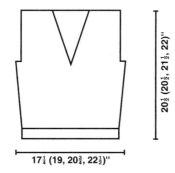

17¼ (19, 20¾, 22½)"

20½ (20½, 21½, 22)"

Directions

Back

With smaller needle, cast on 85 (95, 105, 115) stitches and work twisted rib as follows:

Row 1: (K1tbl, p1) repeat to last stitch, k1tbl.

Row 2: (P1tbl, k1) repeat to last stitch, p1tbl.

Work a total of 14 rows in twisted rib.

Change to larger needle and begin body shaping:

Work 5 rows in stockinette stitch.

Row 6 (WS): P3, increase 1 stitch, work to last 3 stitches, increase 1 stitch, p3.

Repeat these last 6 rows until you have 95 (105, 115, 125) stitches total.

Work straight in stockinette stitch until piece measures 11 (11, 12, 12½)" from the cast-on edge.

Shape armholes:

Bind off 6 (7, 8, 8) stitches at the beginning of the next 2 rows.

Next row: Slip 1 purlwise, k1, ssk, work to the last 4 stitches, k2tog, k2.

Next row: Slip 1 purlwise, p to end.

Work these 2 rows 6 (7, 8, 8) times total.

Work straight until piece measures 19½ (19½, 20½, 21)" from the cast-on edge.

Shape shoulders:

Bind off 6 (7, 8, 9) stitches at the beginning of the next 6 rows.

Bind off 35 (35, 35, 39) back neck stitches.

Front

Work as for back, including all shaping, and *at the same time* when piece measures 12":

Begin neck shaping:

On next row, work to the center stitch and place the center stitch on holder, attach another ball of yarn and work across row. Working both sides at once, decrease 1 stitch at each neck edge every 2 rows 12 times, then every 3 rows 5 times.

Continue straight until piece measures 19½ (19½, 20½, 21)" from the cast-on edge.

Shape shoulders:

Work shoulder shaping to correspond with back.

Finishing

Sew front and back pieces together at shoulders.

Form armhole edgings:

With smaller size needle and right side facing you, pick up 108 stitches around armhole edge. Work in twisted rib (k1tbl, p1) for ¾". Bind off loosely in ribbing.

Make the neckband:

With smaller size needle and right side facing you, pick up 35 (35, 35, 39) stitches from back neck, 41 stitches down left front neck edge, place a center marker, pick up 1 stitch from holder, 41 stitches from right front neck edge, place an end-of-round marker—118 (118, 118, 122) stitches.

Join and work in twisted ribbing (k1tbl, p1) to within 2 stitches of center marker, ssk, slip marker, k1tbl, k2tog, work in twisted ribbing to end of round.

Repeat this round for approx. ¾". Bind off loosely in ribbing.

Weave in all loose ends and steam-press your work lightly from the wrong side. Sew up the side seams.

Speaking of silk (we were just now, weren't we?), I recently dipped into my stash and pulled out a glorious DK-weight silk I bought at a knitting retreat. I had 1,000 yards of this beautiful stuff, and decided to design and knit a shawl. Following are the results of that experiment: the Grape Arbor Shawl.

Grape Arbor Shawl

Approximate Finished Size

90" across

46" down to center point

Materials

9 skeins (100yd/50g) DK-weight silk yarn from the Spirit Trail (www.spirit-trail.net)

US size 8 (5mm) 24 or 36" circular and double-pointed needles

Gauge

4.5 sts and 6 rows = 1" on size 8 needles.

The gauge is not crucially important here. If your gauge is slightly tighter, you will end up with a slightly smaller shawl. Conversely, if your gauge is looser, your shawl will be bigger. You can also control the finished size of your shawl to a certain extent by your blocking.

Note

The entire pattern for the shawl is written out in words. For those of you who prefer to knit lace from a chart, I am including charts for each of the three sections. The first section, the Bunches of Grapes, is charted through row 62. Also please note that only half a row is charted. When you reach the end of the chart, start again at the beginning of the chart for that row to knit the second half of the row.

After you have knitted a few rows, you may find it easier to follow along the written instructions until you memorize the lace pattern. The pattern repeat is very simple, and essentially, all you are doing is adding pattern repeats to your work as soon as you have increased enough stitches to accommodate another whole pattern repeat.

The second section is made up of Vine Lace. All the rows of Vine Lace are written out, and a chart of the pattern repeat only is included.

The chart for the Leaf Edging consists of 8 rows that you will repeat until you have edged the entire shawl.

Directions

Cast on 10 stitches onto your circular needle.

Row 1: K across.

Row 2: P across.

Row 3: K2, yo, k2, yo, k2, yo, k2, yo, k2—14 sts.

Row 4 and all even-numbered rows: K2, p to last 2 stitches, k2.

Row 5: K2, yo, k4, yo, k2, yo, k4, yo, k2—18 sts.

Row 7: K2, yo, k6, yo, k2, yo, k6, yo, k2—22 sts.

Row 9: K2, yo, k8, yo, k2, yo, k8, yo, k2—26 sts.

Row 11: K2, yo, k10, yo, k2, yo, k10, yo, k2—30 sts.

Row 13: K2, yo, k12, yo, k2, yo, k12, yo, k2—34 sts.

Bunches of Grapes

Row 15: K2, yo, k4, k2tog, yo, k1, yo, ssk, k5, yo, k2, yo, k4, k2tog, yo, k1, yo, ssk, k5, yo, k2—38 sts.

Row 17: K2, yo, k4, k2tog, yo, k3, yo, ssk, k5, yo, k2, yo, k4, k2tog, yo, k3, yo, ssk, k5, yo, k2—42 sts.

Row 19: K2, yo, k6, k2tog, yo, k1, yo, ssk, k7, yo, k2, yo, k6, k2tog, yo, k1, yo, ssk, k7, yo, k2—46 sts.

Row 21: K2, yo, k2, k2tog, yo, k1, yo, ssk, k5, k2tog, yo, k1, yo, ssk, k3, yo, k2, yo, k2, k2tog, yo, k1, yo, ssk, k5, k2tog, yo, k1, yo, ssk, k3, yo, k2—50 sts.

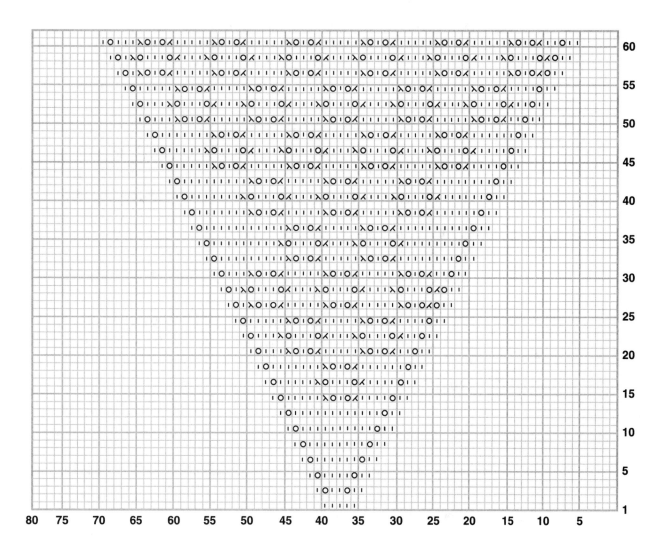

Row 23: K2, yo, k2, k2tog, yo, k3, yo, ssk, k3, k2tog, yo, k3, yo, ssk, k3, yo, k2, yo, k2, k2tog, yo, k3, yo, ssk, k3, k2tog, yo, k3, yo, ssk, k3, yo, k2—54 sts.

Row 25: K2, yo, k4, k2tog, yo, k1, yo, ssk, k5, k2tog, yo, k1, yo, ssk, k5, yo, k2, yo, k4, k2tog, yo, k1, yo, ssk, k5, k2tog, yo, k1, yo, ssk, k5, yo, k2—58 sts.

Row 27: K2, yo, (k2tog, yo, k1, yo, ssk, k5) 2 times, k2tog, yo, k1, yo, ssk, k1, yo, k2, yo, (k2tog, yo, k1, yo, ssk, k5) 2 times, k2tog, yo, k1, yo, ssk, k1, yo, k2—62 sts.

Row 29: K2, yo, (k2tog, yo, k3, yo, ssk, k3) 2 times, k2tog, yo, k3, yo, ssk, k1, yo, k2, yo, (k2tog, yo, k3, yo, ssk, k3) 2 times, k2tog, yo, k3, yo, ssk, k1, yo, k2—66 sts.

Row 31: K2, yo, k2, (k2tog, yo, k1, yo, ssk, k5) 2 times, k2tog, yo, k1, yo, ssk, k3, yo, k2, yo, k2, (k2tog, yo, k1, yo, ssk, k5) 2 times, k2tog, yo, k1, yo, ssk, k3, yo, k2—70 sts.

Row 33: K2, yo, k8, k2tog, yo, k1, yo, ssk, k5, k2tog, yo, k1, yo, ssk, k9, yo, k2, yo, k8, k2tog, yo, k1, yo, ssk, k5, k2tog, yo, k1, yo, ssk, k9, yo, k2—74 sts.

Row 35: K2, yo, k8, k2tog, yo, k3, yo, ssk, k3, k2tog, yo, k3, yo, ssk, k9, yo, k2, yo, k8, k2tog, yo, k3, yo, ssk, k3, k2tog, yo, k3, yo, ssk, k9, yo, k2—78 sts.

Row 37: K2, yo, k10, k2tog, yo, k1, yo, ssk, k5, k2tog, yo, k1, yo, ssk, k11, yo, k2, yo, k10, k2tog, yo, k1, yo, ssk, k5, k2tog, yo, k1, yo, ssk, k11, yo, k2—82 sts.

Row 39: K2, yo, k6, (k2tog, yo, k1, yo, ssk, k5) 2 times, k2tog, yo, k1, yo, ssk, k7, yo, k2, yo, k6, (k2tog, yo, k1, yo, ssk, k5) 2 times, k2tog, yo, k1, yo, ssk, k7, yo, k2—86 sts.

Row 41: K2, yo, k6, (k2tog, yo, k3, yo, ssk, k3) 2 times, k2tog, yo, k3, yo, ssk, k7, yo, k2, yo, k6, (k2tog, yo, k3, yo, ssk, k3) 2 times, k2tog, yo, k3, yo, ssk, k7, yo, k2—90 sts.

Row 43: K2, yo, k8, (k2tog, yo, k1, yo, ssk, k5) 2 times, k2tog, yo, k1, yo, ssk, k9, yo, k2, yo, k8, (k2tog, yo, k1, yo, ssk, k5) 2 times, k2tog, yo, k1, yo, ssk, k9, yo, k2—94 sts.

Row 45: K2, yo, k4, (k2tog, yo, k1, yo, ssk, k5) 3 times, k2tog, yo, k1, yo, ssk, k5, yo, k2, yo, k4, (k2tog, yo, k1, yo, ssk, k5) 3 times, k2tog, yo, k1, yo, ssk, k5, yo, k2—98 sts.

Row 47: K2, yo, k4, (k2tog, yo, k3, yo, ssk, k3) 3 times, k2tog, yo, k3, yo, ssk, k5, yo, k2, yo, k4, (k2tog, yo, k3, yo, ssk, k3) 3 times, k2tog, yo, k3, yo, ssk, k5, yo, k2—102 sts.

Row 49: K2, yo, k6, (k2tog, yo, k1, yo, ssk, k5) 3 times, k2tog, yo, k1, yo, ssk, k7, yo, k2, yo, k6, (k2tog, yo, k1, yo, ssk, k5) 3 times, k2tog, yo, k1, yo, ssk, k7, yo, k2—106 sts.

Row 51: K2, yo, k2, (k2tog, yo, k1, yo, ssk, k5) 4 times, k2tog, yo, k1, yo, ssk, k3, yo, k2, yo, k2, (k2tog, yo, k1, yo, ssk, k5) 4 times, k2tog, yo, k1, yo, ssk, k3, yo, k2—110 sts.

Row 53: K2, yo, k2, (k2tog, yo, k3, yo, ssk, k3) 4 times, k2tog, yo, k3, yo, ssk, k3, yo, k2, yo, k2, (k2tog, yo, k3, yo, ssk, k3) 4 times, k2tog, yo, k3, yo, ssk, k3, yo, k2—114 sts.

Row 55: K2, yo, k4, (k2tog, yo, k1, yo, ssk, k5) 4 times, k2tog, yo, k1, yo, ssk, k5, yo, k2, yo, k4, (k2tog, yo, k1, yo, ssk, k5) 4 times, k2tog, yo, k1, yo, ssk, k5, yo, k2—118 sts.

Row 57: K2, yo, (k2tog, yo, k1, yo, ssk, k5) 5 times, k2tog, yo, k1, yo, ssk, k1, yo, k2, yo, (k2tog, yo, k1, yo, ssk, k5) 5 times, k2tog, yo, k1, yo, ssk, k1, yo, k2—122 sts.

Row 59: K2, yo, (k2tog, yo, k3, yo, ssk, k3) 5 times, k2tog, yo, k3, yo, ssk, k1, yo, k2, yo, (k2tog, yo, k3, yo, ssk, k3) 5 times, k2tog, yo, k3, yo, ssk, k1, yo, k2—126 sts.

Row 61: K2, yo, k2, (k2tog, yo, k1, yo, ssk, k5) 5 times, k2tog, yo, k1, yo, ssk, k3, yo, k2, yo, k2, (k2tog, yo, k1, yo, ssk, k5) 5 times, k2tog, yo, k1, yo, ssk, k3, yo, k2—130 sts.

Row 63: K2, yo, k8, (k2tog, yo, k1, yo, ssk, k5) 4 times, k2tog, yo, k1, yo, ssk, k9, yo, k2, yo, k8, (k2tog, yo, k1, yo, ssk, k5) 4 times, k2tog, yo, k1, yo, ssk, k9, yo, k2—134 sts.

Row 65: K2, yo, k8, (k2tog, yo, k3, yo, ssk, k3) 4 times, k2tog, yo, k3, yo, ssk, k9, yo, k2, yo, k8, (k2tog, yo, k3, yo, ssk, k3) 4 times, k2tog, yo, k3, yo, ssk, k9, yo, k2—138 sts.

Row 67: K2, yo, k10, (k2tog, yo, k1, yo, ssk, k5) 4 times, k2tog, yo, k1, yo, ssk, k11, yo, k2, yo, k10, (k2tog, yo, k1, yo, ssk, k5) 4 times, k2tog, yo, k1, yo, ssk, k11, yo, k2—142 sts.

Row 69: K2, yo, k6, (k2tog, yo, k1, yo, ssk, k5) 5 times, k2tog, yo, k1, yo, ssk, k7, yo, k2, yo, k6, (k2tog, yo, k1, yo, ssk, k5) 5 times, k2tog, yo, k1, yo, ssk, k7, yo, k2—146 sts.

Row 71: K2, yo, k6, (k2tog, yo, k3, yo, ssk, k3) 5 times, k2tog, yo, k3, yo, ssk, k7, yo, k2, yo, k6, (k2tog, yo, k3, yo, ssk, k3) 5 times, k2tog, yo, k3, yo, ssk, k7, yo, k2—150 sts.

Row 73: K2, yo, k8, (k2tog, yo, k1, yo, ssk, k5) 5 times, k2tog, yo, k1, yo, ssk, k9, yo, k2, yo, k8, (k2tog, yo, k1, yo, ssk, k5) 5 times, k2tog, yo, k1, yo, ssk, k9, yo, k2—154 sts.

Row 75: K2, yo, k4, (k2tog, yo, k1, yo, ssk, k5) 6 times, k2tog, yo, k1, yo, ssk, k5, yo, k2, yo, k4, (k2tog, yo, k1, yo, ssk, k5) 6 times, k2tog, yo, k1, yo, ssk, k5, yo, k2—158 sts.

Row 77: K2, yo, k4, (k2tog, yo, k3, yo, ssk, k3) 6 times, k2tog, yo, k3, yo, ssk, k5, yo, k2, yo, k4, (k2tog, yo, k3, yo, ssk, k3) 6 times, k2tog, yo, k3, yo, ssk, k5, yo, k2—162 sts.

Row 79: K2, yo, k6, (k2tog, yo, k1, yo, ssk, k5) 6 times, k2tog, yo, k1, yo, ssk, k7, yo, k2, yo, k6, (k2tog, yo, k1, yo, ssk, k5) 6 times, k2tog, yo, k1, yo, ssk, k7, yo, k2—166 sts.

Row 81: K2, yo, k2, (k2tog, yo, k1, yo, ssk, k5) 7 times, k2tog, yo, k1, yo, ssk, k3, yo, k2, yo, k2, (k2tog, yo, k1, yo, ssk, k5) 7 times, k2tog, yo, k1, yo, ssk, k3, yo, k2—170 sts.

Row 83: K2, yo, k2, (k2tog, yo, k3, yo, ssk, k5) 7 times, k2tog, yo, k1, yo, ssk, k3, yo, k2, yo, k2, (k2tog, yo, k3, yo, ssk, k5) 7 times, k2tog, yo, k1, yo, ssk, k3, yo, k2—174 sts.

Row 85: K2, yo, k4, (k2tog, yo, k1, yo, ssk, k5) 7 times, k2tog, yo, k1, yo, ssk, k5, yo, k2, yo, k4, (k2tog, yo, k1, yo, ssk, k5) 7 times, k2tog, yo, k1, yo, ssk, k5, yo, k2—178 sts.

Row 87: K2, yo, (k2tog, yo, k1, yo, ssk, k5) 8 times, k2tog, yo, k1, yo, ssk, k1, yo, k2, yo, (k2tog, yo, k1, yo, ssk, k5) 8 times, k2tog, yo, k1, yo, ssk, k1, yo, k2—182 sts.

Row 89: K2, yo, (k2tog, yo, k3, yo, ssk, k5) 8 times, k2tog, yo, k1, yo, ssk, k1, yo, k2, yo, (k2tog, yo, k3, yo, ssk, k5) 8 times, k2tog, yo, k1, yo, ssk, k1, yo, k2—186 sts.

Row 91: K2, yo, k2, (k2tog, yo, k1, yo, ssk, k5) 8 times, k2tog, yo, k1, yo, ssk, k3, yo, k2, yo, k2, (k2tog, yo, k1, yo, ssk, k5) 8 times, k2tog, yo, k1, yo, ssk, k3, yo, k2—190 sts.

Row 93: K2, yo, k8, (k2tog, yo, k1, yo, ssk, k5) 7 times, k2tog, yo, k1, yo, ssk, k9, yo, k2, yo, k8, (k2tog, yo, k1, yo, ssk, k5) 7 times, k2tog, yo, k1, yo, ssk, k9, yo, k2—194 sts.

Row 95: K2, yo, k8, (k2tog, yo, k3, yo, ssk, k5) 7 times, k2tog, yo, k1, yo, ssk, k9, yo, k2, yo, k8, (k2tog, yo, k3, yo, ssk, k5) 7 times, k2tog, yo, k1, yo, ssk, k9, yo, k2—198 sts.

Row 97: K2, yo, k10, (k2tog, yo, k1, yo, ssk, k5) 7 times, k2tog, yo, k1, yo, ssk, k11, yo, k2, yo, k10, (k2tog, yo, k1, yo, ssk, k5) 7 times, k2tog, yo, k1, yo, ssk, k11, yo, k2—202 sts.

Row 99: K2, yo, k6, (k2tog, yo, k1, yo, ssk, k5) 8 times, k2tog, yo, k1, yo, ssk, k7, yo, k2, yo, k6, (k2tog, yo, k1, yo, ssk, k5) 8 times, k2tog, yo, k1, yo, ssk, k7, yo, k2—206 sts.

Row 101: K2, yo, k6, (k2tog, yo, k3, yo, ssk, k5) 8 times, k2tog, yo, k1, yo, ssk, k7, yo, k2, yo, k6, (k2tog, yo, k3, yo, ssk, k5) 8 times, k2tog, yo, k1, yo, ssk, k7, yo, k2—210 sts.

Row 103: K2, yo, k8, (k2tog, yo, k1, yo, ssk, k5) 8 times, k2tog, yo, k1, yo, ssk, k9, yo, k2, yo, k8, (k2tog, yo, k1, yo, ssk, k5) 8 times, k2tog, yo, k1, yo, ssk, k9, yo, k2—214 sts.

Row 105: K2, yo, k4, (k2tog, yo, k1, yo, ssk, k5) 9 times, k2tog, yo, k1, yo, ssk, k5, yo, k2, yo, k4, (k2tog, yo, k1, yo, ssk, k5) 9 times, k2tog, yo, k1, yo, ssk, k5, yo, k2—218 sts.

Row 107: K2, yo, k4, (k2tog, yo, k3, yo, ssk, k5) 9 times, k2tog, yo, k1, yo, ssk, k5, yo, k2, yo, k4, (k2tog, yo, k3, yo, ssk, k5) 9 times, k2tog, yo, k1, yo, ssk, k5, yo, k2—222 sts.

Row 109: K2, yo, k6, (k2tog, yo, k1, yo, ssk, k5) 9 times, k2tog, yo, k1, yo, ssk, k7, yo, k2, yo, k6, (k2tog, yo, k1, yo, ssk, k5) 9 times, k2tog, yo, k1, yo, ssk, k7, yo, k2—226 sts.

Row 111: K2, yo, k2, (k2tog, yo, k1, yo, ssk, k5) 10 times, k2tog, yo, k1, yo, ssk, k3, yo, k2, yo, k2, (k2tog, yo, k1, yo, ssk, k5) 10 times, k2tog, yo, k1, yo, ssk, k3, yo, k2—230 sts.

Row 113: K2, yo, k2, (k2tog, yo, k3, yo, ssk, k5) 10 times, k2tog, yo, k1, yo, ssk, k3, yo, k2, yo, k2, (k2tog, yo, k3, yo, ssk, k5) 10 times, k2tog, yo, k1, yo, ssk, k3, yo, k2—234 sts.

Row 115: K2, yo, k4, (k2tog, yo, k1, yo, ssk, k5) 10 times, k2tog, yo, k1, yo, ssk, k5, yo, k2, yo, k4, (k2tog, yo, k1, yo, ssk, k5) 10 times, k2tog, yo, k1, yo, ssk, k5, yo, k2—238 sts.

Row 117: K2, yo, (k2tog, yo, k1, yo, ssk, k5) 11 times, k2tog, yo, k1, yo, ssk, k1, yo, k2, yo, (k2tog, yo, k1, yo, ssk, k5) 11 times, k2tog, yo, k1, yo, ssk, k1, yo, k2—242 sts.

Row 119: K2, yo, (k2tog, yo, k3, yo, ssk, k5) 11 times, k2tog, yo, k1, yo, ssk, k1, yo, k2, yo, (k2tog, yo, k3, yo, ssk, k5) 11 times, k2tog, yo, k1, yo, ssk, k1, yo, k2—246 sts.

Row 121: K2, yo, k2, (k2tog, yo, k1, yo, ssk, k5) 11 times, k2tog, yo, k1, yo, ssk, k3, yo, k2, yo, k2, (k2tog, yo, k1, yo, ssk, k5) 11 times, k2tog, yo, k1, yo, ssk, k3, yo, k2—250 sts.

Row 123: K2, yo, k to center 2 sts, yo, k2, yo, knit to last 2 st, yo, k2—254 sts.

Vine Lace

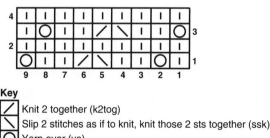

Key

/	Knit 2 together (k2tog)
\	Slip 2 stitches as if to knit, knit those 2 sts together (ssk)
O	Yarn over (yo)
I	Knit (k) on right side, purl (p) on wrong side

Row 125: K2, yo, k4, (k1, yo, k2, ssk, k2tog, k2, yo) 13 times, k3, yo, k2, yo, k4, (k1, yo, k2, ssk, k2tog, k2, yo) 13 times, k3, yo, k2—258 sts.

Row 127: K2, yo, k5, (yo, k2, ssk, k2tog, k2, yo, k1) 13 times, k4, yo, k2, yo, k5 (yo, k2, ssk, k2tog, k2, yo, k1) 13 times, k4, yo, k2—262 sts.

Row 129: K2, yo, k6, (k1, yo, k2, ssk, k2tog, k2, yo) 13 times, k5, yo, k2, yo, k6, (k1, yo, k2, ssk, k2tog, k2, yo) 13 times, k5, yo, k2—266 sts.

Row 131: K2, yo, k7, (yo, k2, ssk, k2tog, k2, yo, k1) 13 times, k6, yo, k2, yo, k7 (yo, k2, ssk, k2tog, k2, yo, k1) 13 times, k6, yo, k2—270 sts.

Row 133: K2, yo, k8, (k1, yo, k2, ssk, k2tog, k2, yo) 13 times, k7, yo, k2, yo, k8, (k1, yo, k2, ssk, k2tog, k2, yo) 13 times, k7, yo, k2—274 sts.

Row 135: K2, yo, k9, (yo, k2, ssk, k2tog, k2, yo, k1) 13 times, k8, yo, k2, yo, k9 (yo, k2, ssk, k2tog, k2, yo, k1) 13 times, k8, yo, k2—278 sts.

Row 137: K2, yo, k10, (k1, yo, k2, ssk, k2tog, k2, yo) 13 times, k9, yo, k2, yo, k10, (k1, yo, k2, ssk, k2tog, k2, yo) 13 times, k9, yo, k2—282 sts.

Row 139: K2, yo, k11, (yo, k2, ssk, k2tog, k2, yo, k1) 13 times, k10, yo, k2, yo, k11 (yo, k2, ssk, k2tog, k2, yo, k1) 13 times, k10, yo, k2—286 sts.

Row 141: K2, yo, k3, (k1, yo, k2, ssk, k2tog, k2, yo) 15 times, k2, yo, k2, yo, k3, (k1, yo, k2, ssk, k2tog, k2, yo) 15 times, k2, yo, k2—290 sts.

Row 143: K2, yo, k4, (yo, k2, ssk, k2tog, k2, yo, k1) 15 times, k3, yo, k2, yo, k4 (yo, k2, ssk, k2tog, k2, yo, k1) 15 times, k3, yo, k2—294 sts.

Row 145: K2, yo, k5, (k1, yo, k2, ssk, k2tog, k2, yo) 15 times, k4, yo, k2, yo, k5, (k1, yo, k2, ssk, k2tog, k2, yo) 15 times, k4, yo, k2—298 sts.

Row 147: K2, yo, k6, (yo, k2, ssk, k2tog, k2, yo, k1) 15 times, k5, yo, k2, yo, k6 (yo, k2, ssk, k2tog, k2, yo, k1) 15 times, k5, yo, k2—302 sts.

Row 149: K2, yo, k7, (k1, yo, k2, ssk, k2tog, k2, yo) 15 times, k6, yo, k2, yo, k7, (k1, yo, k2, ssk, k2tog, k2, yo) 15 times, k6, yo, k2—306 sts.

Row 151: K2, yo, k8, (yo, k2, ssk, k2tog, k2, yo, k1) 15 times, k7, yo, k2, yo, k8 (yo, k2, ssk, k2tog, k2, yo, k1) 15 times, k7, yo, k2—310 sts.

Row 153: K2, yo, k9, (k1, yo, k2, ssk, k2tog, k2, yo) 15 times, k8, yo, k2, yo, k9 (k1, yo, k2, ssk, k2tog, k2, yo) 15 times, k8, yo, k2—314 sts.

Row 155: K2, yo, k10, (yo, k2, ssk, k2tog, k2, yo, k1) 15 times, k9, yo, k2, yo, k10 (yo, k2, ssk, k2tog, k2, yo, k1) 15 times, k9, yo, k2—318 sts.

Row 157: K2, yo, k11, (k1, yo, k2, ssk, k2tog, k2, yo) 15 times, k10, yo, k2, yo, k11, (k1, yo, k2, ssk, k2tog, k2, yo) 15 times, k10, yo, k2—322 sts.

Row 159: K2, yo, k3, (yo, k2, ssk, k2tog, k2, yo, k1) 17 times, k2, yo, k2, yo, k3 (yo, k2, ssk, k2tog, k2, yo, k1) 17 times, k2, yo, k2—326 sts.

Row 161: K2, yo, k4, (k1, yo, k2, ssk, k2tog, k2, yo) 17 times, k3, yo, k2, yo, k4, (k1, yo, k2, ssk, k2tog, k2, yo) 17 times, k3, yo, k2—330 sts.

Row 163: K2, yo, k5, (yo, k2, ssk, k2tog, k2, yo, k1) 17 times, k4, yo, k2, yo, k5 (yo, k2, ssk, k2tog, k2, yo, k1) 17 times, k4, yo, k2—334 sts.

Row 165: K2, yo, k6, (k1, yo, k2, ssk, k2tog, k2, yo) 17 times, k5, yo, k2, yo, k6, (k1, yo, k2, ssk, k2tog, k2, yo) 17 times, k5, yo, k2—338 sts.

Row 167: K2, yo, k7, (yo, k2, ssk, k2tog, k2, yo, k1) 17 times, k6, yo, k2, yo, k7 (yo, k2, ssk, k2tog, k2, yo, k1) 17 times, k6, yo, k2—342 sts.

Row 169: K2, yo, k8, (k1, yo, k2, ssk, k2tog, k2, yo) 17 times, k7, yo, k2, yo, k8, (k1, yo, k2, ssk, k2tog, k2, yo) 17 times, k7, yo, k2—346 sts.

Row 171: K2, yo, k170, yo, k2, yo, k170, yo, k2—350 sts.

Row 172: K2, p to last 2 stitches, k2.

Leaf Edging

You should have the right side of the shawl facing you. Do not break yarn, and cast on 10 stitches using the backward loop cast-on onto your needle. With a double-pointed needle in the same size as your circular needle, begin the lace edging as follows:

Foundation row: Knit across the 10 stitches you just cast on, knitting the last cast-on stitch together with the first "live" shawl stitch.

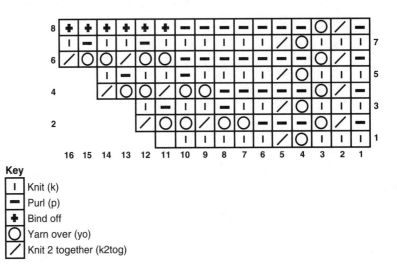

Key

I	Knit (k)
▬	Purl (p)
✚	Bind off
O	Yarn over (yo)
╱	Knit 2 together (k2tog)

Begin leaf edging:

Row 1: K3, yo, k2tog, k5—10 sts.

Row 2: K2tog, yo, yo, k2tog, yo, yo, p3, yo, k2tog, p1tog with next live shawl stitch—12 sts.

Row 3: K3, yo, k2tog, k2, p1, k2, p1, k1—12 sts.

Row 4: K2tog, yo, yo, k2tog, yo, yo, p5, yo, k2tog, p1tog with next live shawl stitch—14 sts.

Row 5: K3, yo, k2tog, k4, p1, k2, p1, k1—14 sts.

Row 6: K2tog, yo, yo, k2tog, yo, yo, p7, yo, k2tog, p1tog with next live shawl stitch—16 sts.

Row 7: K3, yo, k2tog, k6, p1, k2, p1, k1—16 sts.

Row 8: Bind off 6 sts, p7, yo, k2tog, p1tog with next live shawl stitch—10 sts.

Continue knitting the edging onto the shawl, until you are 2 stitches away from the center stitch of the point of the shawl. For the next 5 shawl stitches (the 2 sts leading up to the center stitch, the center stitch, and the 2 sts after it), knit the last stitch of the edging with the shawl stitch every 4th row, rather than on every other row, in order to ease some fullness into the point of the shawl. Continue knitting the lace edging as before until you have knitted up all the live stitches of the body of the shawl. Cast off and weave in any loose ends.

Finishing

You will need to block your shawl. Wet the shawl thoroughly, then gently squeeze out excess water. Pin the shawl out to shape on a bed or on a carpeted floor covered with bath towels or a clean sheet. You may need to re-stretch and repin the shawl to get it to the desired shape and size. Allow the shawl to dry completely before unpinning.

Chapter 11 • What's a Peerie?

I'VE ALWAYS BEEN INTENSELY INTERESTED IN THE HISTORY and traditions of different societies in general. And because I see the world through knitting, historical and traditional knitting, specifically, have always fascinated me.

I've learned a lot by studying the patterns and techniques and colors used in different ethnic knitting. Most of these old patterns are timeless and deserve a place of respect in the great pantheon of knitting. The cross-cultural similarities in patterns often reflect the migrations and invasions of the people.

Different knitting traditions resulted for many reasons and I knit them for many reasons. I am eager to learn the traditional techniques, lose myself in glorious color combinations and interesting textured stitches, and to feel a connection with knitters who have gone before me.

One of my first traditional knitting obsessions was with the British fisher gansey. A gansey is a fisherman's sweater, usually knitted from five-ply worsted wool at a fine gauge. Ganseys are knitted in the round and are usually patterned with complex texture stitches. Different towns and geographical areas were known for different stitch patterns.

In the mid-1980s I first discovered that there was such a thing as a traditional British fisherman's sweater that was not an Aran. I read an article about the gansey in a knitting magazine, back in those long-ago pre-Internet days.

When I saw a photo of a gansey, I became obsessed with it, as per usual. I managed to find books about ganseys, and even a source for the wool from which they were traditionally knit: the fine five-ply worsted wool. The recommended gauge was seven or eight stitches to the inch.

I went all out, as I usually do. I bought the frighteningly long and sharp steel double-pointed needles that in years gone by had typically been used to knit ganseys. I bought the five-ply worsted wool in dark navy blue, the traditional color. I confess that I even bought a "knitting belt": a leather belt stuffed with horsehair that you fastened around your waist, sticking the end of one of your needles into a hole in the contraption. And I knitted a traditional gansey, in the round. Complete with underarm gussets and elaborate textural patterning. However, I never did get the hang of the knitting belt, and abandoned all attempts to use it early on in the process. Still, I do think I ought to get credit for trying. I managed to punch a few holes in my fingers in the knitting process: those long steel double-pointed needles in small sizes are very dangerous! However, I felt very safe when I was wielding those babies in public. Nobody messed with me.

Ten years after I knitted my first gansey, I spent a week in Cornwall. I had never visited there before, and it was a delight to visit places whose names I knew through gansey patterns: Polperro, Mevagissey, Perranporth. The names had always sounded magical to me, and the places themselves, tiny, quaint fishing towns, almost lived up to their magical names. There was one glaring omission: no gansey yarn or patterns anywhere that I could find. And trust me, I looked.

We took a day trip to Tintagel to visit the remains of what is thought by some to be King Arthur's Camelot. Leaving Tintagel, near the town of Padstow, I spied a modest sign at the side of a road that read "Wool Shop."

"Stop the car!" I shrieked to my companion, who, sure I was having a fit of some sort (although at this point he really ought to have known better), quickly pulled over. The shop appeared to be the outlet for a co-op of some sort and I happily purchased some Black Welsh Mountain wool. The friendly and slightly wacky shop assistant weighed out the earthy, gamey-smelling skeins on an old-fashioned scale. I was in wool heaven. But there was not a single traditional pattern to be had in that shop.

This was only one instance in my long history of seeking out patterns and yarn that are indigenous to an area whenever I travel. I am often, sadly, without success. In the mid-1980s I took a trip to the beautiful Loire Valley in France. One morning my traveling companions and I were waiting to tour a stately château. Everyone except me was oohing and aahing over the château. What was I doing? Taking photos of a flock of sheep in an adjoining field. Of course. Next year's French wool crop, on the hoof!

In the mid-to-late 1990s I spent a good deal of time in Wales, a country covered in sheep. I always spent my time in Wales woozy with delight. My long-suffering travel companion would automatically nod and say (in a monotone) "That's nice" every time I pointed to a field of sheep from the car window and gushed: "Ooooooh! Little woolly baa-lambs!"

(He did, at one point, point out to me that cooing at lambs and petting them, and then immediately thereafter going to a pub and having a lamb sandwich for lunch seemed inconsistent. I could think of no reasonable defense for my actions.)

To my surprise and disappointment, there were very few yarn shops, or any tradition of knitting that I could find. Prosaic, commercial yarn was available in a few department stores, but that was it. But hope springs eternal. We drove all over the country (and on some very scary small roads indeed), up very steep hills and down very steep valleys, in my quest for wool. I visited a few small wool mills, but they were mostly geared toward producing wool for weaving. I did manage to buy some wool here and there. Where there's a will, there's a way. Or rather, where there's a mill there's a way. But to this day, I've yet to discover any worthwhile information on Welsh knitting traditions.

Okay, so much for Welsh knitting. I moved on to Fair Isles.

My first Fair Isle, the one that I started by twisting it into a Möbius strip, was a cardigan made from seventeen or eighteen different colors, knitted in the round and steeked.

I never do things the easy way.

The Fair Isle was great fun to knit. All those colors! It kept me interested and entertained to see the color-work pattern emerge. It was educational, too. I learned that the small motifs in Fair Isles are called peeries. I learned about steeks. A steek is nothing more than a vertical panel of stitches added to your knitting to form a section of real estate, if you will, an area that you will cut later to make an opening, on either side of which you can pick up stitches. For example, you can steek the front opening of a cardigan, or the armholes.

When the time came for me to cut open my first steek, I just did it. I sat down and cut it open according to the pattern, then picked up the stitches for the front bands of the cardigan. Ditto for the sleeves. Snip, snip, we have armholes.

It never occurred to me, not even once, that cutting into knitting might be a Bad Thing. It said to do it in the pattern, right? Therefore, it would work. And it did.

Because Shetland wool is a hairy, "sticky" yarn, it does not unravel when you cut into stitches vertically. (Horizontally, however, is a different matter. I would advise you not to try that.) And when you pick up your stitches around the steeked opening—always a few stitches in from the cut edge—that edge always obediently lies down flat on the inside of your knitting and stays there obediently. This never fails to enchant me.

Ignorance is indeed bliss. Years later, I discovered that cutting one's knitting is one of the top ten stress inducers for knitters. Knitters have been known to retreat into darkened rooms with alcoholic beverages to steel themselves for the ordeal of steeking. Who knew?

I will confess here and now that I don't even tack down my steeked edges to the inside of my work after finishing the sweater. I just let them flap in the breeze, as it were. The truth is, I see no need for any finishing. I steam the daylights out of them with my steam iron and, being nice hairy Shetland wool, the steeks stick to the body of the sweater. They wouldn't dream of going anywhere. They wouldn't dare.

Knitting Fair Isles brings us to the "float" versus "weave" debate. To float or to weave? That is the question.

First of all, what am I talking about? When you are working in two colors and have a long stretch of one color, some knitters catch the yarn not in use under the working yarn halfway through to anchor it: a weave. Other knitters do not. They leave the nonworking color loose over the stretch of the other color being worked: a float.

I used to weave. But no longer. Now I float, almost always. Even for long stretches, like ten stitches. As long as I make sure I've got my stitches spread out well on the needle while I knit, I have no problem with tension. I find that weaving sometimes shows on the right side. At least it does when I do it. When working with Shetland wool, floats adhere to the back side of the work with no problem, so you don't have a bunch of messy loops like you might think. Remember: hairy and sticky.

Now, if you were knitting a color-work sweater for a small child you might want to weave on the back, to prevent little fingers from getting stuck in the floats when you are dressing the child. One good yank with a finger inside a loop and you've got a disaster.

Another big color-work controversy: do you knot and cut or weave in the ends?

One of the drawbacks of doing color work (at least in my mind) is that you're left with approximately fifty billion ends from all the color changes.

Weaving in all those ends can be a very arduous task. I used to stop every couple of inches and devote some time to carefully weaving in ends on the wrong side of my work. If you are knitting a cardigan, it is much easier: you start and stop each color in the middle of your front steek, so you can just trim off the ends when you cut open the steek. However, you still have to deal with the ends on the sleeves.

One day someone asked me if I weave in my ends or knot them and cut them off. I confess that knotting and cutting had never occurred to me. But it sounded like a great idea. From that point on, I would take the two ends—the color just ended and the color just started—and knot them together in a square knot, then trim the ends to about a quarter of an inch.

At first I was concerned that the knots would, well, unknot, but square knots are stubborn little things. Particularly after you steam the hell out of them.

When I finish knitting a Fair Isle sweater, it usually looks less than wonderful. It'll have an almost wrinkled look to it. I find that no matter how good my tension is (and my two-color tension is pretty good), I almost never end up with a smooth Fair Isle. I turn to one of my favorite tools: the steam iron. I may have mentioned my love of steam.

I love my steam iron. It smoothes out a multitude of sins.

So I steam the living heck out of my Fair Isles. That steaming, I find, is sufficient to block it into wearable shape. Some people employ a device called a "woolly board" but I don't find that it's necessary.

A woolly board is an adjustable, usually wooden, frame over which you can stretch a dampened knit sweater and leave it to dry to the proper size and shape. It's a great device that works very well, but I'm perfectly happy with my steam iron.

After conquering the Fair Isle (in my own mind, anyway) I moved on to Shetland lace knitting.

My first Shetland lace knitting project (and pretty much my first lace of any sort) was a wedding handkerchief, a piece of lace knitted using Shetland shawl construction techniques, using cobweb-weight Shetland wool, knitted on size 00000 needles.

Did I mention that I never do things the easy way?

This was a great experience. The pattern for this handkerchief was in a compilation of patterns from around the world, a book put out by one of the textile magazines I subscribed to, *Threads*. In the process of knitting this, I learned a lot of things: traditional Shetland lace patterns, how a Shetland lace shawl is constructed, and how to block lace. I relearned that those steel needles in tiny sizes are excruciatingly sharp. I also happened to sprain my wrist while blocking that piece of lace within an inch of its life. Every time I look at it today, I get a twinge in my wrist.

Then I moved on to Norwegian knitting.

I am pleased to report that knitting is alive and well in Norway. There are all sorts of beautiful patterns based on traditional designs readily available. Norwegian sweaters are also knit in the round and steeked, but they employ a slightly different steeking technique from Fair Isle knitting. You don't cast on any extra stitches—you just knit a big tube for the body and then, using a sewing machine, run lines of stitching down the sides where you want your armholes and cut between the lines of machine stitching.

When you knit the sleeve, in the round, you start at the cuff and knit up to the top, increasing stitches to increase the circumference as you go. Once the sleeve is the desired length, you knit a facing of about an inch before casting off.

I discovered that the Norwegian steek can frighten people almost as much as the Fair Isle steek. But the Norwegian steek is not nearly as scary as it sounds, honest!

Here's what you do:

When you have finished knitting your sweater body and are casting off the shoulders, put a pin at the top of each side seam to help you find it later. Steam-block the pieces and lay them out. Your pattern may tell you the armhole depth, but you should use this as a guide only. If your tension varies slightly, your armhole will need to be shallower or deeper. Measure the sleeve top right before the facing to get its height. Now use that measurement to mark the armhole depth on the body and put a pin at the point where the sleeve will end. Put another pin in the same spot on the other side.

Next, stitch the steek area on the body using a sewing machine. This is the area four stitches wide where you will cut open the armholes. Use regular sewing thread and a straight stitch with normal tension. I find it helpful to stitch the steeks with a thread color that's slightly different from the color of the sweater so you can see your stitching lines.

Starting at the top of the sweater, machine-stitch down to just past your pin, turn and stitch a couple of stitches at a right angle, then turn and stitch back up to the top. Repeat this process half a stitch out from the first line of stitching, so you have double stitching all the way around your armhole. Repeat this process on the other side for the other armhole.

Next comes the fun part: cutting!

With a sharp pair of scissors, carefully cut open your armhole in the center between the two rows of stitching. Stop cutting just before the turned stitching at the bottom. Be careful not to cut into the machine stitching.

Assembling the sweater is easy. Sew your shoulder seams together. Set in the sleeves by pinning the sleeve into the armhole, remembering that the facing goes to the inside, and sew the sleeve in, using your usual sewing method. Then sew down the facings invisibly on the inside.

Obviously, Norwegian sweaters weren't always done this way, but I suppose before the invention of the sewing machine they were hand-stitched. Typically, the yarn used for Norwegian knits is not as sticky and hairy as Shetland wool, so you need some sort of reinforcement to keep those cut stitches from going nuts and unraveling with reckless abandon.

I've happily knit lots of Norwegian designs, and even designed my own Norwegian sweater, sized for babies, the "Baby Norgi," which is available as a free pattern online at knitty.com.

The one thing that annoyed me about the Norwegian designs that I've knitted is that the pattern usually directs you to begin knitting back and forth when you start knitting the neck shaping. I hate knitting stranded color work back and forth—purling in two colors is tedious at best. So I devised my own way of doing the neck shaping on Norwegian knits, using steeks.

Because I've elected to do a neckline steek rather than knit back and forth, I always have to alter the neckline decreases a bit. The pattern directs you to cast off a given number of stitches for the center of the neck on the first row, then to decrease some number of stitches (i.e., more than one stitch) on subsequent rows to shape the slope of the neck.

Well, you can't quite do it this way with a steek. You can decrease one stitch at a time on either side of the neck steek on each row. So that's what I do until I get the proper number of decreases. Yes, it does alter the shape of the neck slightly, but not enough to make a difference, in my opinion. I've done this on most of the Norwegian sweaters I've made without any problem.

While it can be fun to try the different techniques used in traditional knitting, I usually opt for the easiest and most efficient way of getting something done. As long as my finished sweater looks the way I want it to look, and is constructed so that it won't fall apart, I'm happy. With all my slipshod cutting, nonweaving, knotting ways, I've yet to make a sweater using these techniques that hasn't stood the test of time.

I love my Norgi sweaters, but because I have Swedish ancestry, I have an ongoing interest in finding out everything I can about traditional Swedish knitting. Apart from one book published in the 1990s, I couldn't find any information in English on traditional Swedish knitting.

I love the Internet.

My online knitting buddy Johanne, who lives in Stockholm, is also interested in historical Swedish knitting. She has sent me a couple of books (in Swedish, of course) about knitting that include a lot of traditional pattern motifs. Pay dirt!

I set out to design a traditional Swedish sweater. Most of the museum piece Swedish sweaters I've seen were knitted at an insanely tiny gauge—some of them upward of ten stitches per inch. Because I wanted to finish my sweater in my lifetime, I designed mine at the gauge of eight stitches to the inch. And because I'm a rebel, a bad-ass knitter if you will, I knitted my design using a very untraditional yarn: Koigu KPPPM. I used only two colors: a solid and a variegated. I used a traditional Swedish motif that I saw on a photograph of a sweater knitted in the 1800s. The results are quite pleasing to the eye, I think, and give the garment a look of complexity, while it is actually rather simple to knit. A bonus is that Koigu KPPPM knits like a dream, although you could use any fingering-weight yarn that gives you the proper gauge. A less experienced knitter who is not afraid to try something new (like cutting steeks!) could manage this, even though it is knit at a fine gauge. But I think an experienced knitter will enjoy it as well.

While it employs mostly traditional methods of Scandinavian knitting, I've written the pattern so that the neck shaping is achieved using steeks, because that's how I like to make mine. Just call it my own little twist on a traditional sweater.

I call the sweater "Ingrid," in cherished memory of my Swedish paternal grandmother, Ingrid Frantz Johansson.

Ingrid Pullover

Finished Measurements

37 (42, 48)" chest
23 (24, 25)" length

Materials

Color A (background): 6 (7, 9) skeins Koigu KPPPM monochrome color (100% wool, 175yd/50g skein)
Color B: 5 (6, 8) skeins Koigu KPPPM variegated color
US size 0 (2mm) and size 1 (2.5mm) 16" and 32" circular needles (or size to get gauge)
US size 0 (2 mm) and US size 1 (2.5mm) double-pointed needles (or size to get gauge)

Gauge

32 sts and 38 rows = 4" measured over stockinette stitch using size 1 needles

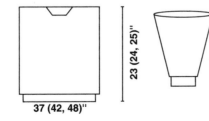

pattern repeat

Directions

Body

You will knit the body in the round in one piece.

With smaller size 32" circular needle and Color A, cast on 294 (338, 382) stitches. Join, being careful not to twist stitches. Place a marker at the beginning of the round and after stitch 147 (169, 191). Work stockinette stitch (knit every row) for 7 rounds to create a facing. Purl 1 round for the fold line.

Knit 1 round in Color A.

K1 round in Color B.

K2 rounds in Color A.

K1 round in Color B.

K1 round in Color A.

Change to the larger size 32" circular needle and k 1 round in Color B.

Start the chart:

*Knit the first 2 stitches of the chart, repeat the 22 sts of the pattern repeat until 13 stitches before the middle of the round marker, knit the last 13 stitches of the chart; repeat from * once more.

Work the chart until the piece measures 17 (18, 19)" from the fold line.

Shape front neck:

Work the first 51 (62, 71) stitches, place the next 45 (45, 49) stitches on a holder. Alternating the two colors, cast on 10 stitches (1 edge stitch, 8 steek stitches, 1 edge stitch). Work to the end of the round.

Keeping the chart pattern correct, decrease 1 stitch at each front neck edge (outside the edge stitch) 5 times, then on alternate rounds 5 times.

At the same time, when the piece measures 22 (23, 24)" from the fold line, shape the back neck.

Shape back neck:

Work straight around the front.

Pattern across 45 (56, 65) stitches of the back.

Place the next 57 (57, 61) stitches on a holder. Alternating the two colors, cast on 10 stitches (1 edge stitch, 8 steek stitches, 1 edge stitch). Work to the end of the round.

Keeping the chart pattern correct, decrease 1 stitch at each back neck edge (outside the edge stitch) 4 times.

Work until 23 (24, 25)" from the fold line.

With Color A, graft or knit the shoulders together.

Sleeves

With smaller size double-pointed needles and Color A, cast on 81 stitches. Join, place marker. Work stockinette stitch (knit every row) for 7 rounds to create a facing. Purl 1 round for the fold line.

Knit 1 round in Color A.

K1 round in Color B.

K2 rounds in Color A.

K1 round in Color B.

K1 round in Color A.

Change to the larger size double-pointed needles and k1 round in Color B.

Start the chart:

Knit the first 2 stitches of the chart, repeat the 22 sts of the pattern repeat until 13 stitches before the end-of-round marker, knit the last 13 stitches of the chart.

Increase 1 stitch at the beginning and end of every 4th round 38 (40, 42) times, leaving 2 stitches between increase stitches and working increased stitches into the pattern until you have a total of 157 (161, 165) stitches (switching to a circular needle when you have enough stitches). At the same time, when the sleeve measures 17 (17½, 18)" from the fold line, work 1 round in Color B, then work 2 rounds in Color A. Purl 6 rounds in Color A for the facing and cast off.

Finishing

Set in the sleeves:

Lightly steam the body and the sleeves. Lay the sleeves flat and measure the depth just inside the purl facing. Mark the armhole depth on the body and put a pin at the point where the sleeve will end. Put another pin in the same spot on the other side.

Next, create the steeks by machine-stitching the body in each armhole area using a sewing machine. Sew 2 rows of machine stitching down each side, across the bottom, and up the other side of the 4-stitch-wide area of each armhole steek.

With a sharp pair of scissors, carefully cut open your armhole in the center between the 2 rows of stitching. Stop cutting just before the turned stitching at the bottom. Be careful not to cut into the machine stitching.

Sew your shoulder seams together and then set in the sleeves. Pin the sleeve into the armhole and sew the sleeve in from the right side, making sure that the machine stitching on the body is inside the seam. On the sleeve, sew through the last stitch before the purl facing, keeping the facings on the inside. Sew the facings down invisibly on the inside. Steam-press the armhole seams and the facings.

Make the neckband:

Cut open the front and back neck steeks, between the fourth and fifth steek stitches. With Color A and the smaller size 16" circular needle, pick up and knit 8 stitches per inch around the neck.

Knit 1 round in Color A.

K1 round in Color B.

K2 rounds in Color A.

K1 round in Color B.

K1 round in Color A.

Purl 1 round in Color A.

Knit 7 rounds in Color A for the facing and cast off knitwise.

Sew the sleeve and body hems:

Fold the bottom and sleeve facings to the inside and sew down invisibly. Weave in all loose ends and steam-press the hems and sleeve seams.

Chapter 12 • Putting a Spin on It

FOR YEARS I HARBORED A SECRET DESIRE TO LEARN HOW TO SPIN.

It all started over twenty years ago. My then mother-in-law offered me spinning lessons as a birthday or holiday gift (I can't remember exactly which). And after I learned how to spin, she was going to buy me a spinning wheel. Sadly, these gifts never materialized. I don't remember why (once again, my memory fails me on the details), but ever since then I've felt a mild disappointment about the whole spinning business.

That disappointment was resurfacing and nagging at me more frequently since I started reading knitting blogs. A lot of knit bloggers spin. They write in their blogs about spinning. I read their blogs. The result? I yearn to spin. It's simple cause and effect.

I am very impressionable.

However, I also know that I am compulsive. My yarn stash threatens to take over my living space and I couldn't help but wonder what would happen if I amassed a stash of unspun fiber. So I resisted the idea of spinning for a couple of years.

But still, reading about other people's spinning and seeing photos of the lovely yarns they created was a huge temptation for me.

In the autumn of 2004, something snapped. I'm not sure what it was. Most likely it was my last thread of self-control. I woke up one morning and thought, "I am going to learn how to spin."

I bullied my friend Lindsey-Brooke (a good and patient soul), who has been spinning for over twenty years, into attempting to teach me. We were planning on attending a knitters' and spinners' retreat the first weekend in November, so that seemed like a perfect time to start.

I mentioned on my blog that I wanted to learn how to spin and asked my readers for their recommendations for a drop spindle for a beginner. After considering all their advice, I bought the one that most people seemed to think would be best, a Bosworth Midi. A kind reader sent me a box of samples of different rovings (fibers prepared for spinning by carding so that all the fibers are smoothed out), each in its own plastic bag, neatly marked to identify the contents.

I know a lot of knitters and spinners who are incredibly generous. They are also great enablers.

The first Friday in November I set out for the retreat, which was held at a lodge in the mountains of Virginia. I was all ready: I had packed my car full of knitting, fiber, my drop spindle, and all the accompanying paraphernalia. Along with the requisite bottles of tequila, Cointreau, vodka, and Kahlúa. And plastic cups and swizzle sticks.

My motto? Be prepared.

It was a beautiful autumn day, perfect for a drive in the country. I arrived at the lodge in great spirits, and not-so-great voice, having sung along very loudly (and very off-key) with the Beatles CDs I was playing in the car.

Lindsey-Brooke was there when I arrived, sitting on the tailgate of her truck in the parking lot, knitting of course. We registered and went immediately to our room to unpack. After a quick lunch of smoked salmon and Irish cheese that Lindsey-Brooke had brought and Black Russians courtesy of my traveling bar (we do know how to do things with style), we took out the drop spindles.

I should point out here that I had, a couple of weeks previous, halfheart-edly attempted to teach myself to use the drop spindle according to some writ-ten instructions. With disastrous results, naturally.

This did not surprise me. I know that I am a very impatient person, never wanting to take the time to actually read instructions. I took a quick look at the directions I had and immediately whipped out some fiber to slop onto the spindle. The results were—you guessed it—slop. I ended up with a twisted mess of fiber that would give sheep nightmares. My cat Lucy seemed enter-tained by it, though. Disgusted, I put everything aside until I could try again with my private tutor.

On my first attempt, with Lindsey-Brooke's coaching, I actually made yarn. It was thick, bulbous, gloppy, horrific, uneven, icky yarn, but it was yarn nonetheless. I was beyond thrilled. Lindsey-Brooke showed me how to ply the singles together to make a two-ply yarn. After half an hour or so of spinning, I had a repulsive, uneven little skein of yarn that only a mother could love. And love it I did!

My next skein of yarn was much more even (though still amateurish). I felt drunk with success. (I'm sure the vodka had nothing to do with it.)

At this point we needed to take a break from spinning to attend some re-treat activities. But after the day's events were done, we went back to the room to drink margaritas and spin. Lindsey-Brooke had ordered two sampler boxes of fiber from a yarn and fiber supplier, and we went through the boxes, spin-ning the samples.

Some of the samples spun like a dream; some gave me fits. Soy silk? I am quite certain that soy silk and I will never coexist peacefully, unless it has already been spun into yarn by someone else. It is a demon fiber.

I was still having trouble making my spindle actually spin. But perhaps drinking margaritas and spinning until two thirty in the morning might have something to do with that.

The next day we got to shop at the vendors' market at the retreat. One vendor had some pretty Kundert spindles for sale. Lindsey-Brooke suggested, "Why don't you try one of those?" I picked out one with a pretty inlay design that seemed nicely balanced and bought it.

And wowie, wow, wow! It spun like a dream! My spinning improved one hundred percent using this new spindle. One flick of the wrist and it seemed to spin forever. We spent another evening spinning away, well into the night.

On Sunday afternoon I headed home, my car packed with yarn and fiber purchases. I had already begun on the path to fiber stashdom. One of the vendors was selling her fiber out of the back of her van right before we left, giving the whole operation an illicit, alluring, somewhat naughty air. I easily gave in to my urge to purchase some. Okay, I purchased more than "some." I purchased mass quantities of fiber.

Upon arriving home Sunday night, I hauled everything inside my condo as quickly as possible. I had had the great good sense to take the next day off from work, so I happily spun more of the samples and plied them until the wee hours.

Lindsey-Brooke had told me that in order to set the twist in my new yarn, I needed to soak the skeins in warm soapy water, rinse it, and hang it up to dry with a weight on the bottom. It wasn't long before the back of my bathroom door was hung with little skeins of yarn, weighted down with metal S-hooks, dripping on the towels I had put on the floor.

A fine addition to my already dubious decor.

Over the next couple of weeks I shopped online for fiber. Large lightweight boxes started arriving every day. I bought a beautiful handmade spindle with a lovely sunflower carved on the whorl. I took my spindle and some fiber to work with me every day and spun during my lunch hour. And I talked about it all on my blog.

My blog readers started wondering how soon it would be before I bought a spinning wheel. I laughed and said I was perfectly happy with my drop spindle. All I wanted to be able to do, I said, was spin small amounts of exotic fibers to knit little projects. However, even as I was writing this on my blog, I didn't fully believe it. The little voice in my head kept insisting, "You'll cave in and buy a wheel. It's just a matter of time."

I knitted a catnip mouse for my cat Lucy, out of an alpaca/merino/silk blend yarn I spun from samples sent to me from an online buddy. It quickly became Lucy's favorite toy and she all but loved it to death. It was true, I thought, giftees really do appreciate the extra time and care you put into gifts knitted from your own handspun yarn. Imagine that! I knitted a little pouch from a wool/silk blend and sent it to Lindsey-Brooke as a thank-you gift.

I happily continued to spin on my spindle. I didn't want a wheel. I was far too uncoordinated to be able to work a wheel, I reasoned (trying to convince myself).

But . . . it wouldn't hurt to look at photos of wheels online. . . .

We all know where this is headed, right? Two weeks to the day after I learned how to spin on a drop spindle, my wheel was delivered.

This wheel is a Kromski Minstrel, a castle wheel beautifully made with lovely turnings. I had named her before she arrived: Katarina.

I do have the habit (I think it is charming though others no doubt call it childish or weird) of naming inanimate objects. The wheel just looked like a Katarina to me. But my cell phone looked like a Victor to me, so go figure.

Ian and I carried the large box that Katarina came in up to my condo and I lovingly unpacked the pieces. She, of course, came unassembled, with not only illustrated assembly instructions, but a video. However, I did not watch the video until two days after assembling her. I like to do things the hard way.

We got Katarina assembled in an hour or so. There she stood, in all her pristine elegant glory. I worked her treadles a few times but didn't attempt to spin until after I watched the video because I was unclear exactly how one spins on a spinning wheel.

The first chance I got, I popped the video in the player and expectantly sat down at my wheel with some roving in hand. Most of the video dealt with assembly of the various wheels the company makes, but there was a brief "how to spin" section at the end. Enlightenment at last!

I learned how to thread the leader yarn using the orifice hook. (I still think that "orifice hook" sounds like a medieval instrument of torture. I suppose it could be used thusly, but I swear I've only used it to thread yarn on a spinning wheel. Honest.) And away I went! I was spinning in no time. And I was amazed at how easy it was. No doubt those two weeks of drop spindling served me in good stead. Or perhaps I knew how to spin in a previous life. Whatever the reason, I was happily spinning along, and creating yarn that actually looked like yarn.

Herein lies the path to madness. I had been buying fiber from online vendors. Now I started searching online auctions as well for unspun fiber. It delighted me that unspun fiber is quite a bit cheaper than yarn. Though I'm not sure why this never occurred to me. After all, with unspun fiber, one has to do all the work oneself, right?

I bought all sorts of exotic fibers. Baby camel, cashmere, yak down, and guanaco. I am not sure what a guanaco is, but, apart from qiviut, I will tell you that it is the loveliest, softest fiber I've ever had the joy to have and hold. I then found unspun qiviut for sale in an online auction, so of course I bought that, too.

And I bought silk, and wool, of course. I happily bought a lot of dyed wool, but I've always loved undyed wool so I bought a lot in natural colors as well: whites, grays, and browns.

Then I got it into my head that it would be really cool to spin a whole bunch of natural-colored wools and knit a simple shawl out of them, striping the different colors randomly. Lindsey-Brooke had brought such a shawl she had knitted from her handspun yarn to the retreat and I had admired it. It was beautiful.

L-B wrote down her simple "shawl formula" for me—a formula that, she pointed out, was no doubt not her original thought, but nonetheless a good way to knit a simple shawl.

It goes like this:

Cast on 5 stitches.

Row 1 (right side): Knit 1, yarn over, knit 3, yarn over, knit 1. You now have 7 stitches on your needle.

Row 2 (and all wrong side rows): Purl across.

Row 3: Knit 1, yarn over, knit 1, yarn over, knit 3, yarn over, knit 1, yarn over, knit 1. You now have 11 stitches on your needle.

Row 5: Knit 1, yarn over, knit 3, yarn over, knit 3, yarn over, knit 3, yarn over, knit 1. You now have 15 stitches on your needle.

You can see where this is headed, right? You keep increasing 1 stitch at both the beginning and the end of each increase row, as well as 1 stitch on either side of its center 3 stitches. And you continue to knit until the shawl is as long as you'd like it to be. Or until you pass out from the boredom of it all.

I started spinning up my natural wools into a yarn that I hoped would be worsted weight. I had but a single ounce of some fibers and two to four ounces of others. When I had about half the fiber spun, plied, skeined, and washed, I started knitting. Using a US size 8 (5mm needle), I cast on my 5 stitches and started knitting.

It was great fun at first. I varied the width of the stripes and alternated between light and dark colors. The contrast looked a bit stark and frighteningly ugly at first, but as the shawl grew, it started to look better. It wasn't long before I had to take my work off the twenty-four-inch needle and transfer it to a forty-inch needle.

Reaching the point of utter boredom happily coincided with my running out of yarn. I had four ounces of Black Welsh Mountain wool/alpaca blend left, and I used it to make a fringe for the bottom edge. I cannot begin to describe how terrifying it is to cut up your own handspun yarn, sweated and toiled over, into short lengths for fringe. I had labored long and hard to create this skein of yarn. And now I was going to slash it into pieces? It seemed so wrong.

But I sucked it up, and cut the yarn into fringe. Magically, the skein was just the right size to make the proper amount of fringe for the bottom edge. I think I owe a lot to dumb luck. I steamed the living daylights out of the shawl, fringed it, and carefully spread it on the floor for its photo op.

Lucy, of course, immediately claimed it as her own, and I had to admit that it matched her seal point coloring quite nicely. Still, I took it away from her after a brief but ugly power struggle, and took it to the office and hung it on the back of my desk chair. It is my emergency warmth shawl for those days when our heating is less than adequate. Or when the air-conditioning is overexuberant.

I learned a lot from this project. I impressed the heck out of myself by actually spinning all those different wools (I believe there were sixteen varieties that went into the shawl) to about the same weight yarn. Like I said, dumb luck! And all the yarns are fairly evenly spun, although they do have that lovely handspun look. I'll say it again: dumb luck.

I was also surprised that the pieces of yarn I cut, in my frenzy of agony, to make the fringe actually stayed pieces of yarn and didn't regress into a fuzzy tangled mass of fibers. Lindsey-Brooke taught me well: always set the twist in your newly spun yarn by washing and then hanging your weighted skeins to dry. (I hesitate to tell you, however, that after teaching me that, she admitted to me that she doesn't always do so herself.)

So I continue to spin merrily along. Like most things in life, I suppose, you can get really technical and scientific about the mechanics of spinning. This is no doubt a good thing, and paying close attention to twists per inch and drive ratios and other mysterious things undoubtedly makes for a better finished project. But at this point, I don't pay too much attention to things like that. I am blissful in my ignorance, and the stuff that's coming off my wheel doesn't look too bad. It knits up fairly well and the knitted fabric hasn't shown any signs of deterioration or pilling. So I'm happy. It's not brain surgery. What's the worst that will happen if I mess up? I'll kill some roving.

And, as one of my online friends is wont to say, "It's the process." I love the process. I look forward all day to coming home and sitting down at the wheel to spin. I love the rhythm I get into when working the treadles. And I love the feeling of the fiber running through my fingers as I spin it into yarn.

And furthermore, I think it is extremely cool to have learned such an ancient craft, something that people have been doing in one form or another for thousands of years. And I appreciate the irony that a good deal of what I learned about spinning I learned from doing research on the Internet. My spinning wheels are now permanent fixtures in my living room, just a few feet away from my laptop computer, which is connected to the Internet via a wireless network. It is a nice juxtaposition of high-tech and low-tech, I think.

Did you notice that I said "spinning wheels," plural? Exactly thirty-one days after ordering my first spinning wheel, I ordered my second wheel. I now have a Lendrum folding wheel: Lenny.

I use both wheels. Lenny has modern streamlined good looks and is as quiet as a whisper when I spin on him. Katarina has old-world beauty and charm. When I spin on her, there are gentle creaks and squeaks, and she actually meows when she needs oil. Often I will spin singles on Lenny and ply them on Katarina. Then everyone can be involved.

Shortly after Lenny arrived, I spun some 100% silk roving on him, and plied the singles into a worsted-weight yarn on Katarina. The roving color was described as "Autumn Splendor" and I had just two ounces of it. I decided to make a phone cozy for my cell phone, Victor. This is a great quick project, perfect for using small bits of exotic fiber and for when you need to make a swell last-minute gift. It can be completed in an hour or two, depending on your knitting speed.

Silk Cell Phone Cozy

Materials

2 ounces of worsted-weight silk or other fiber

1 button

Double-pointed needles (set of five) to get gauge

Gauge

4.5 stitches to the inch measured over stockinette stitch.

This pattern fits a small flip phone. You can easily resize it for a different-size phone.

Directions

Cast on 5 stitches. Working back and forth on two of the dpns, work in garter stitch for 1½". Cast off all stitches, but do not break the yarn.

Pick up 8 stitches along one of the long sides, 4 stitches across one end, 8 stitches along the other long side, and 4 stitches along the other end, for a total of 24 stitches. Divide these stitches onto 4 of the dpns as follows: 8, 4, 8, 4.

Join and work in the round in stockinette stitch (knit every round) until your work measures 3½" from the point where you picked up stitches (or until it is tall enough to almost come to the top of your phone when you slip it inside).

Work in knit 2 purl 2 rib for two rounds, then cast off in knit 2 purl 2 rib. Pick up 4 stitches in the center of the top edge on one of the long sides. Using two needles, work back and forth in garter stitch until the garter stitch piece extends over the top of the phone and a short distance down the other side.

On the next row, ssk, k2tog, so that you have 2 stitches left. Work an I-cord on these 2 stitches until you have a cord long enough to fashion a button loop, then cast off. Sew the end of the I-cord back to the beginning of the cord to form the loop. Weave in all loose ends of yarn. Try the cozy on your phone and mark the front of it for proper placement of the button, then sew the button on.

Another quick and easy project for handspun yarn is a pair of fingerless mitts. I've been buying small quantities—about two ounces each—of lovely hand-dyed merino wool roving and spinning them up into a heavy worsted-weight yarn, at about 100 yards per two ounces. I made the mitts with about 80 yards, in one day. If you are not a spinner, you could substitute any heavy worsted yarn. Either Noro Kureyon or Noro Silk Garden would substitute nicely.

Fingerless Mitts

Size

To fit a woman's medium hand

Materials

Approximately 80 yards of heavy worsted-weight yarn
US size 8 (5mm) double-pointed needles (set of five), or size to get gauge

Gauge

4 sts to the inch measured over stockinette stitch on size 8 needles

Directions

Cast on 28 stitches, divided over four needles.

Join and work in the round in k2 p2 rib for 16 rounds.

Next round: *K2tog, k5; repeat from * to end of round—24 stitches remain.

Knit the next 3 rounds.

Start thumb gusset:

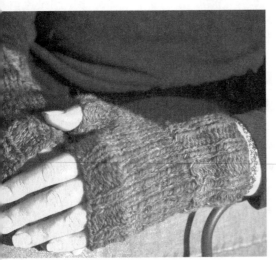

Round 1: K1, place marker, make a stitch by picking up a loop between the stitch you just knit and the next stitch and knitting into that loop, k1, make a stitch, place marker, knit to the end of the round.

Round 2: Knit.

Repeat these 2 rounds until you have 11 stitches in between the markers. Knit 3 rounds further.

Finish the "body":

Next round: K1, remove marker, place the next 11 stitches on a length of yarn, cast on 2 stitches using the backward loop method, remove marker, knit to the end of the round.

Knit 4 more rounds, decreasing 1 stitch over the 2 cast-on stitches over the thumbhole on the last round.

Work k2 p2 rib for 8 rounds and bind off.

Finish the thumb:

Place 11 stitches from holder on dpns and knit across them, pick up 4 stitches from the cast-on stitches—divide stitches evenly over dpns.

Next round: Knit 11, k2tog twice.

Next round: (K1, p1) to last 2 stitches, p2tog.

Work in k1 p1 rib for 3 more rounds, then cast off in rib.

I made these mitts in one day. I started the first one on the morning commute, finished it on my lunch hour, started the second one then, and finished it on the commute home. This is a great project for a last-minute gift.

So, I continue to spin, and view the world from a spinner's perspective. I have briefly considered attempting to spin all sorts of odd things: dryer lint, the cotton I pull out of vitamin bottles, my own hair. The truth is, I have spun my own hair, though not intentionally. Here's a tip: When you are spinning and have longish hair, do not lean forward unless your hair is tied back. Ouch.

When my cat is sitting in my lap, I run my fingers through her long fur and think about shaving her, and spinning her fur. Then I could knit her a little sweater to wear from her own fur.

I would never do that. That would be wrong.

Abbreviations

beg	beginning
cn	cable needle
dec	decrease
dpns	double-pointed needles
inc	increase
k	knit
k2tog	knit 2 sts together
k3tog	knit 3 sts together
p	purl
p2tog	purl 2 sts together
psso	pass slipped stitch over
RS	right side
sl	slip
ssk	slip 2 stitches individually to the right-hand needle as if to knit, knit those 2 stitches together
st	stitch
sts	stitches
tbl	through back loops
tog	together
WS	wrong side
yo	yarn over

Glossary of Terms

Acrylic A nonnatural fiber yarn, touted as a miracle fiber in years gone by because of its ability to stand up to hard wear and repeated machine washings; also able to withstand plague and pestilence.

Alpaca An adorable critter with a cute face, related to the llama. The alpaca has lovely lightweight silky wool that is a joy to spin and knit.

Angora A soft fuzzy fiber that comes from bunnies.

Aran yarn Slightly heavier than worsted weight, Aran-weight yarn is usually knit at 4 to 4.5 stitches to the inch.

Baby yarn Not infant yarn that needs to mature; rather, yarn used to make items for babies, usually knit at 7 to 8 stitches to the inch. Also called *fingering yarn*.

Ball of yarn What you want to wind your yarn into before commencing knitting with it. Also an epithet or exclamation: "Great balls of yarn!"

Binding off See CASTING OFF.

Bulky yarn Heavier than chunky weight, usually knit at a gauge of 1.5 to 2.5 stitches to the inch.

Cable A design motif made by crossing a stitch or group of stitches over (or under) another stitch or group of stitches.

Cable needle A short double-pointed needle used to hold stitches in the making of a cable.

Cashmere The Cadillac of knitting fibers, softer and warmer than wool. Cashmere comes from cashmere goats.

Casting off Finishing a piece of completed knitting in a way that keeps the stitches from unraveling. There are many different methods of casting off. Also called *binding off* or *fastening off*.

Casting on Putting stitches on the needle to begin a project. There are many different methods of casting on.

Chain A crochet stitch that creates, not surprisingly, a chain. I use a crocheted chain for a provisional cast-on when making toe-up socks.

Chunky yarn Heavier than Aran-weight yarn, usually knit at a gauge of 3 to 3.5 stitches to the inch.

Circular needle A knitting needle that has two needle points connected by a cable that can vary in length. You use a circular needle to knit in the round, creating a tube, but you can also use a circular needle to knit flat, back and forth.

Cotton Knitting fiber derived from the cotton plant. Pure cotton has very little elasticity and tends to stretch and sag over time.

Crochet hook The tool used to crochet, also helpful for picking up dropped stitches in knitting.

Decrease To reduce the number of stitches in your work; used to shape a piece of knitting. There are a number of different decreasing methods.

Double knitting (or DK-weight) yarn A light worsted-weight yarn, generally knit at about 5.5 stitches to the inch.

Double-pointed needles Straight needles with a point at each end, double-pointed needles are used to knit in the round and create a tube, like a sock. They are sold in sets of four or five.

Duplicate stitch An embroidery stitch that imitates the knitted stitch. You can duplicate-stitch over a knitted fabric in a different color to make a design (or to cover an error, with no one the wiser). Also called *Swiss darning*.

Fastening off See CASTING OFF.

Fingering yarn See BABY YARN.

Flat knitting As opposed to circular knitting, working the stitches across the right side of a piece, turning it over, and working across the wrong side of the piece. This creates a flat piece of knitting rather than a tube.

Garter stitch In flat knitting, garter stitch is achieved when you knit every row. In circular knitting, you would knit one row, purl one row.

Gauge The number of stitches and rows in your knitting, usually measured per inch or a given number of centimeters. Also called *tension*.

Grafting Invisibly joining two rows of knitting together, for example, at the toe of a sock. Also called *Kitchener stitch*.

Graph A chart with symbols that represent stitches.

Increase To add stitches in your work; used to shape a piece of knitting. There are a number of different increasing methods.

Kitchener stitch See GRAFTING.

Knit The basic stitch in knitting. A knit stitch is formed by inserting the needle into an existing loop, from left to right, and pulling a strand of yarn through to form a new loop.

Knitwise Execute as if to knit; for example, "slip 1 stitch knitwise."

Make one To increase a stitch in knitting. You can make one by picking up the bar between two stitches and knitting into it, or by working into the front and back of one stitch, or by casting on or knitting on a stitch at the end of a row.

Mohair A soft fuzzy fiber that comes from mohair goats. Some folks think it is itchy, but I think it is heavenly.

Pass slipped stitch over A method of decreasing; slip one stitch, work the next stitch, then pass the slipped stitch over the one just worked and drop it off the needle.

Pattern diagram A schematic that shows the basic size and shape of the pieces that make up a knitted garment.

Pick up stitches Knit (or purl) into the loops along the edge of a piece of knitting to make an edging, for example, a neckband.

Purl The "back side" of a knit stitch. A purl stitch is formed by inserting the needle into an existing loop, from right to left, and pulling a strand of yarn through to form a new loop.

Purlwise Execute as if to purl; for example, "slip 1 stitch purlwise."

Qiviut The Rolls-Royce of fibers, qiviut is the downy undercoat of the arctic musk ox. It is extremely soft, light, and warm. Not to mention extremely expensive.

Reverse stockinette stitch In flat knitting, knit one row, purl one row. In circular knitting, purl every row. This differs from stockinette stitch in that the purl side is the right side.

Right side The outside, or "public" side of a piece of knitting.

Silk A fiber derived from the cocoons of the very industrious silkworm. Silk does not have a lot of elasticity and garments knit from it can stretch and sag. It has a beautiful sheen and drape, however, and blended with wool it makes a lovely, more durable yarn.

Skein One of the ways that yarn is "bundled" for sale—you must usually wind a skein into a ball before using it.

Slip Move a stitch from one needle to another without working it. Usually you slip a stitch "as to knit" if you are knitting, and "as to purl" if you are purling.

Sock yarn Sock yarn is generally the same weight as baby (or fingering) yarn, with a gauge of approximately 8 stitches per inch, and it often has some percentage of nylon in its makeup for added strength and durability.

Sport-weight yarn Usually knitted at a gauge of around 6 stitches to the inch.

Stash A common phenomenon among knitters. The stash is a knitter's reserve store of yarn. Some knitters dip deep into their stashes often and willingly to use for projects; others hoard their stashes like a secret treasure.

Steek A group of stitches cast on at the beginning of the armholes (or at the center front of a circularly knit sweater if you are making a cardigan) that will be cut into to make the sleeve openings (or the front opening in the event of a cardigan).

Stitch holder A device used to hold stitches that are not currently being knitted. For example, you may want to put the stitches for the center of the neck of a sweater on a holder while you shape each side of the neck.

Stockinette stitch In flat knitting, knit one row, purl one row. In circular knitting, knit every row.

Tension See GAUGE.

Wool Fiber from that most noble of animals, the sheep.

Worsted-weight yarn Slightly heavier than DK weight, usually knit at about 5 stitches to the inch.

Wrong side The inside, or "private" side of a piece of knitting.

Yarn over Create a new stitch by wrapping the yarn over the right-hand needle.

Resources

Cables Without a Cable Needle—my tutorial on knitting cables without a cable needle, complete with photos: http://wendyknits .net/knit/cablelesson.htm

Capital Animal Care—an animal rescue organization located in Arlington, Virginia; these wonderful people are the ones who rescued my lovely cat Lucy and made it possible for her to come live with me: http://www.capitalanimalcare.org

Fearless Fair Isle Project—my beginners' Fair Isle project, complete with pattern and color charts: www.wendyjohnson.net/fairisle /index.htm

Knit Happens—purveyors of lovely yarns, patterns, needles, and accessories, along with a full complement of knitting and crochet classes year-round; located at 127A North Washington Street, Alexandria, VA 22314, and online at www.knithappens.net

The Knitlist—an e-mail list for sharing knitting questions and content worldwide: http://groups.yahoo.com/group/knitlist/

Knitting Blogs Web Ring— http://boogaj.typepad.com/knitting_blogs/

Knitty—quarterly online knitting magazine with excellent free patterns and articles: http://knitty.com

Petfinder—adopt a pet and help an animal shelter rescue a puppy or kitten: www.petfinder.org

Spirit Trail Fiberworks—source for lovely hand-dyed yarns (the source for the silk yarn used in my Grape Arbor shawl pattern) and spinning fiber, online at: www.spirit-trail.net/

WendyKnits—my website, including my daily knitting blog, gallery of finished work, and free patterns and tips: http://wendyknits.net